More Praise for *The Custom-Fit Workplace*

"Finally, a book that provides busy managers the tools they need to match today's workplace to the needs of today's workforce. Joan Blades and Nanette Fondas not only explain the business logic behind this need, they provide concrete guidance to help you redesign jobs—from executive to file clerk—to attract and keep the best talent out there."—Joan C. Williams, Distinguished Professor of Law, 1066 Foundation Chair and director, Center for WorkLife Law, University of California, Hastings College of the Law, and author, *Reshaping the Work-Family Debate*

"*The Custom-Fit Workplace* tackles an issue that affects all of us: How to work and have a life in the 21st century? A compelling mix of stories, research, and 'how to', this book proves the irrefutable truth that creating a flexible 'custom fit' between work and life is a win for both business and people."—Cali Williams Yost, CEO, Flex+Strategy Group, and author, *Work+Life*

"*The Custom-Fit Workplace* deals with the supply side of the work-life flexibility debate, an area which is often underexamined. Filled with best practices, this book will help employers take the lead in moving beyond policy adoption to implementation."—Dr. Ellen Ernst Kossek, University Distinguished Professor, Michigan State University, School of Human Resources and Labor Relations, and coauthor, *CEO of Me*

"*The Custom-Fit Workplace* is replete with innovations that our parents would have found astonishing and our kids will find self-evident. In a series of brilliant practical suggestions, Joan Blades and Nanette Fondas show how to create a workplace in which investing in workers' dignity pays off in performance and profits."—Robert W. Fuller, author, *Somebodies and Nobodies* and *All Rise*

The Custom-Fit Workplace

The Custom-Fit Workplace

Choose When, Where, and How to Work and Boost Your Bottom Line

Joan Blades
Nanette Fondas

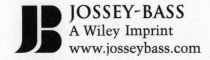
JOSSEY-BASS
A Wiley Imprint
www.josseybass.com

Published by Jossey-Bass

A Wiley Imprint

989 Market Street, San Francisco, CA 94103–1741—www.josseybass.com

Jossey-Bass books and products are available through most bookstores. To contact Jossey-Bass directly call our Customer Care Department within the U.S. at 800–956–7739, outside the U.S. at 317–572–3986, or fax 317–572–4002.

Jossey-Bass also publishes its books in a variety of electronic formats. Some content that appears in print may not be available in electronic books.

Library of Congress Cataloging-in-Publication Data

Blades, Joan.
  The custom-fit workplace : choose when, where, and how to work and boost your bottom line / Joan Blades, Nanette Fondas. — 1st ed.
    p. cm.
  Includes bibliographical references and index.
  ISBN 978-0-470-63353-3
  1. Flexible work arrangements. 2. Work—Social aspects. 3. Quality of work life.
I. Fondas, Nanette, 1959- II. Title.
  HD5109.B53 2010
  650.1'1—dc22

                                                                                    2010015673

Printed in the United States of America
FIRST EDITION
HB *Printing*   10 9 8 7 6 5 4 3 2 1

Contents

The Custom-Fit Workplace

1

WORK IS NOT WORKING

The Case for The Custom-Fit Workplace

Anita, David, and Jake have a problem. They are also on the verge of a discovery.

Anita's long day starts at 5:30 AM, when she wakes to get herself ready for work and her two children for school. She drops the kids off at 7:30 and barely makes it to work by 8. She works nonstop all day, frequently eating lunch at her desk. At 5 PM, she leaves to pick up the kids, make dinner, help with their homework (when did fourth grade get so hard?), do laundry, check for messages from teachers and friends, prepare lunch boxes, and put out any fires that start—hurt feelings from bickering kids, a stuffed dog's broken tail, an unusually high electric bill. By the end of the day, after the kids are bathed and put to bed, she is tapped out. Within minutes of hitting the pillow, she's asleep, though not always at rest, because she often wakes up and thinks about unresolved issues—the conflict with a coworker, her son's difficulty learning to read, the upcoming doctor's appointment she may have to reschedule. The family needs Anita's income, but she's not sure she can keep this up. She already has frequent colds because she's so run-down, and arguments with her husband and kids are increasing right along with her stress level.

David's office is down the hall from Anita's cubicle. David understands Anita's plight because he gave his time, indeed his life, to his career and to his company's success. He wishes he'd spent more time with his kids, but when he has regrets, he reminds himself that his kids came out fine, went to great colleges, and aren't beginning their adult lives saddled with debt. The sacrifice he made seems worth it, though he is troubled to see his son, Jake, now penalized by his employer for making a different choice. Jake was just passed over for a promotion because he chose to be home for dinner with his family during the week instead of putting in late nights. It bothers David that Jake's talent goes underutilized because he is unwilling to work sixty-hour weeks.

Even so, David feels torn when one employee asks to come in at 10 AM and stay late to avoid traffic or another asks to work part time in order to take a continuing education class. He's read a lot about companies that offer some flexibility, but he's accustomed to a clearly defined workday and touching base with his staff by popping into their work space. It's friendly. He likes to see his employees busy at their stations, ask questions, and evaluate their work on the spot. It's easy to judge commitment that way, by seeing who gets there first or who stays late to finish a project. David hates to mess with success—but he can see that Anita, his top producer, is exhausted and unhappy. He doesn't want to lose her, and it's been on his mind because Jake has told him he's so disappointed in his employer he's started looking for another job.

Anita, David, and Jake's problem is one that too many of us face: workplace requirements and job demands that are too rigid, extreme, or unyielding—in terms of how, when, and where work gets done; how job and career ladders are designed; and how life's other important obligations are met. They sense—as most of us do—that there are better ways to work together to improve both business results and people's lives.

With solid information and some inspiration, Anita, David, and Jake are on the verge of discovering that job and personal responsibilities do not have to collide. Work, family, life goals and aspirations, civic participation, physical health, and other parts of life they treasure can be an energizing mix rather than a tug-of-war. They are about to discover that workplace demands *can* be compatible with the rest of their lives. They can have a *custom fit.*

Not Your Grandparents' Workplace

Work is not working. This is Anita's problem, David's problem, Jake's problem—this is our problem. But how did we get here?

Imagine taking your grandparents to work with you for a day. Some elements would look familiar to them. The rigid expectations, for instance, of time in the office, promotion requirements, and visibility, are all too often the same as they were decades ago. Yet they'd also see that the colleagues, technology, and pace of work have profoundly changed.

Gone is the "organization man" who worked traditional hours while his wife stayed home to care for children full time. The number of two-earner households has grown, mostly out of economic necessity, but also out of a growing desire for professional fulfillment. Fifty percent of the workforce is now made up of women; two-thirds of women with children under six are in the workforce.[1]

Since it's no longer the norm that a wife stays home, she's often doing double duty. But she's not the only one. The squeeze demonstrated by Anita's story also applies to David's son, Jake. Indeed, in the 2008 National Study of the Changing Workforce, *fathers* reported more work-life conflict than ever before: in 1977, only 35 percent said they experienced some or a lot of conflict, but by 2008, 59 percent did.[2]

Caregiving responsibilities don't end there. "[Don't forget] the uncle watching over his injured niece coming back from Afghanistan. Or the father taking in his father to look after him," says Deborah Frett, CEO of the Business and Professional Women's Foundation.[3] Nationwide, 30 million families provide care for an adult family member or friend, and according to demographic trends, that number will rise.[4] So will the number of workers juggling care of *both* children and elders.[5] Moreover, while a rising number of workers are busy caring for others, very few workers overall are engaged in caring for themselves—health, personal time, relationships, parenthood are all losing out to the greater pull of endless office hours, snarled commutes, and after-hours e-mail and text messages. Roles and responsibilities have changed, and so have the makeup and priorities of the workforce. Immigrant workers, older workers, and disabled workers, all with varying backgrounds and concerns, are occupying the offices, cubicles, and line positions now. To be sure, today's workforce is a vibrant, diverse group, one with updated ideas about the role of work and a balanced life. Whereas the World War II generation took for granted that if you kept your head down and worked hard, you could consider your life successful, today's workforce has a different mentality—one that asks for more.

Plugging In to the Whole Wide World

Fifty years ago, when workers left for the day, chances were they clocked out and that was that. In today's world, work doesn't end when we shut down our computers and walk away from our desks. Even when not physically in the office, many of us are still plugged in. Smart phones, netbooks, Wi-Fi cafés, texting on-the-run, and other technological advances (which are often not social advances) have made 24/7 availability common for a large swath of the American workforce. For some, this has been liberating. The traditional workday—and workplace—have cracked wide open. Advertisements for the latest e-devices dangle the promise of poolside conference calls and filing a report while lounging on the beach. That's the bright side. The dark reality? Millions of people are hounded by work that follows them wherever they go. The same advances that make it possible to avoid snowy roads by working from home also keep workers awake checking e-mail until three in the morning, or texting colleagues while on the family vacation.

While technology means you can do your job from Bermuda, it may also mean that anyone in Bermuda can do your job. Internet connectivity has caused companies to confront the reality that the entire world is their labor pool. It's a phenomenon Thomas Friedman documents exhaustively in *The World Is Flat:* technology is leveling the playing field between developing and developed nations, remote villages and city centers, young and old, in-the-skyscraper companies and in-the-garage start-ups.[6] The way we work will never be the same again.

A global labor pool changes everything. It means that U.S. companies—which have been hit with shrinking profits—will continue to feel pressure to work more effectively and efficiently. It means that a medical professional in India can read your X-ray, a manufacturing worker in China can print your book, and a customer service center anywhere in the world can take a late-night call about your account balance. For companies in a growing number of fields, the benefits of outsourcing are steadily outweighing its costs, all of which put increasing pressure on U.S. workers to be more and more productive.

Pressure to get fewer people to produce more—to increase productivity—will continue unabated. "How much more can employers squeeze employees without turning off candidates and shedding existing workers?" asks Ira S. Wolfe, author of *The Perfect Labor Storm 2.0.* The limit to productivity is constantly being tested, constantly being pushed.

The thing is, human beings have limits, too.

When the Cup Overflows

Today's work demands spill over into stressed marriages and unhealthy children; they damage our overall health, productivity, and responsibility as citizens and humans. In a 2008 survey by the organization Life Meets Work, employees reported stress and overload from managing multiple priorities—grappling with

factors such as the needs of children and aging relatives, schedules, illness, and job security.[7] And, sadly, recent research from
Harvard University, the Gates Foundation, and the National
Alliance for Caregiving showed poor outcomes for children
resulting from workplace practices that prevent parents from
being good workers and good parents.[8]

Some workers have adjusted to an overflowing cup by reducing or eliminating parts of their home life:[9] having fewer or no
children, getting married later or not at all, or getting divorces.
In families able to get by on one income, one spouse may be
forced out of a much-loved job because the other's work spills
over into private life, making two careers impossible. And make
no mistake—it is not just people with families who are pressured.
According to work-life expert Phyllis Moen, single workers are
feeling stress as a result of overload, time pressures, and the
expectation that they be available anytime, anyplace.[10] We're
constantly being pushed for more, but work conditions have
become toxic. Personal circumstances may exacerbate stress, but
it's the "work" part of the "work-life" equation that is pushing us
all to the edge.

The simple truth is that workplace demands often are not
compatible with the realities of modern life. Change in the
workplace to fit these realities has been slow and stubborn. Why?
Practices like permitting workers to schedule their own flexible
hours, blurring the rigid divide between worker and parent, or
doing away with a physical office require a leap of faith. They
may require leaders to step outside their comfort zones. Yet not
only can such practices deliver the efficiency and productivity
the global marketplace demands, they can allow people to successfully integrate their work and nonwork lives. That's it.
Change doesn't have to require a leap of faith—it can be grounded
in solid research and successful models, making change not only
necessary but good.

As we enter the second decade of the twenty-first century,
we have more ideas and tools than ever before to create effective,

profitable, sustainable business organizations. Yet many organizations have not embraced the opportunity to improve workplace practices. In the United States we are witnessing unprecedented working hours, worker burnout, and a loss of creativity. Far too many people are "working stupid": a condition caused by working excessive hours without adequate rest and rejuvenation (warning: this can lead to serious errors in judgment or simply a lot of wasted time). Something's got to give. We hope it is not ourselves, our families, or our livelihoods.

Introducing Custom Fit

The news from the workplace isn't all bad. Some workplaces *have* changed. Mothers in particular have led the way, demanding new ways of working, initiating and taking advantage of options such as flextime, virtual work, and compressed working hours. Many had no choice but to do things differently. As advocates for mothers and families through our work at MomsRising.org, we've heard inspiring stories of women who've spearheaded this change and of workplaces that are good for people with caregiving responsibilities.

But we recognize that all workers—not just parents—have a set of work and life demands, goals, and obligations that are not limited to family responsibilities. Most people have constraints on their ability to cope with a 24/7 work culture: issues related to health and physical needs, community obligations, and educational aspirations, as well as religious and extended family commitments. We came to this project in part because, while mothers may have played the role of the squeaky wheel, it's really the engine of our workplace that needs to be fixed.

Both employees and employers are hungry for ideas and solutions. Joan knows from many years managing the software company Berkeley Systems and MoveOn.org, the five-million-member grassroots organization, that managers and workers crave knowledge about ways to get work done effectively while at the same time honoring and supporting people's complex lives.[11]

Nanette, too, has long been attuned to the demands and challenges confronting workers and managers. For more than two decades she has taught and written about successful business practices and management approaches, including theories of person-job fit, organization-environment fit, and business-strategy fit. When Nanette became a mother, she saw the problem of work-life fit firsthand. She began to apply her scholarly ideas to the lived experiences of people around her, who freely shared their hopes and dreams of better compatibility between work and home.

Together, we embarked on an exploration of workplace strategies that help people find what we call a *custom fit*—the successful integration of job and personal commitments. But custom fit is not just about employees. Any practice that creates a work-life fit for them has to help employers as well. We have focused on win-wins: ways managers and other leaders can better meet the needs of today's workforce while improving company results and competitiveness.

In the process we learned something extraordinary and hopeful: there doesn't have to be a tug-of-war between job and life commitments. More often than not, what is good for workers is good for the employer. We found that organizations that value the whole worker and accommodate the whole range of needs often benefit greatly. Happier, less stressed workers tend to do stronger work, even *more* work, than their beleaguered colleagues. Not only that, they are unlikely to walk out the door and take their talent elsewhere. They serve customers better and make them want to return. Our search showed us that the workplace can embrace changes to better accommodate *every* worker—from single worker to parent, from aging Baby Boomer to Generation X or Y, and even worker types that have yet to emerge.

For many of us, a workplace that matches our shifting priorities and the changes taking place in our society's demographics, in technology, and in the competitive landscape cannot come fast enough. All we need are two ingredients. First, we need workplace customs better suited to the myriad demands swirling around people in all types of jobs and organizations. These are policies and practices, and organizational designs and job tracks, that allow people to seek—and hopefully achieve—a *custom fit* between their personal set of talents, responsibilities, and needs and the job's demands, constraints, and end products. Second, we need leaders who are willing to try new ways of getting work done and who deeply value each employee's contribution.

This book opens up the dialogue and challenges both people and organizations to make the custom-fit workplace a reality for everyone. And it shares the good news that the alignment of a job's demands with a person's other responsibilities benefits both employers and employees. With a *custom fit*, work can *work* again—for Jake, David, Anita, and all of us.

Making Work Really Work Again

You may already be familiar with companies that offer some flexible work arrangements—methods for tweaking the traditional full-time job—and people who take advantage of them. A flexible work arrangement might include working longer shifts on fewer days a week, cutting back on hours, or working outside of a physical office.

The custom-fit workplace can offer one or more of these options, but it goes a step further still. It asks leaders and organizations to shed the constraints of traditional management approaches and ways of organizing work to focus on two questions:

- What does it take to accomplish the job at hand?
- How can we best accomplish that task while respecting and valuing the worker doing the job?

Cutting-edge practices and models that answer these questions form the backbone of this book:

Virtual work—telecommuting or remote working that goes beyond occasionally "working from home."

On-demand work—tapping into the talent pool of workers who may not want permanent, full-time jobs but will work for an employer on a contract basis, sometimes from home.

Redesigned career tracks—reworking rigid up-or-out career tracks to retain valued workers who otherwise might opt out of the job.

Integrating kids and work—allowing new parents to bring an infant to the workplace for the first six to eight months of life or until the baby is crawling.

High-commitment work practices—empowering workers to take responsibility for their products and the success of their teams.

Almost any job can be made to better fit the worker, if this is a priority for both management and the employee. That said, common sense dictates that particular custom-fit strategies are better suited to specific types of work. Virtual work is an easy fit for jobs that primarily rely upon phone communication or specialized work like programming, writing, or online collaboration. Integrating kids and work can fit in some retail, closed offices, or even sales jobs, but clearly wouldn't fit at a construction site. We do want to encourage you to think beyond what you originally think is possible. Allow the stories and case studies in this book to spur a way of approaching work-life fit that asks Why not? before saying no.

A *custom fit* looks different depending on the person, job, and time of life. Because our lives change dramatically over the course of years, the fit that is needed may change too. University of Minnesota sociologist Phyllis Moen calls this "life-course" fit. A fit at one time may not be a fit later. Milestones such as finding a partner, bearing a child, caring for a parent, starting a business, becoming unemployed, earning a promotion, or reaching retirement age create new conditions that may require a new fit.[12]

Erin's Story

Erin has worked hard to create enviable work-life integration over the years. Her job, family, and other obligations have been aligned and realigned, thanks to her own initiative and a flexible employer who values her contribution. This employer, too, has benefited from Erin's education, training, and loyalty for more than twenty years.

Upon graduation from her master's program in economics, Erin became an entry-level hospital administrator. Life was good—her work was challenging and gratifying, and her personal life flourished with a happy marriage. She was promoted into management; regular salary increases rewarded her dedication and expertise. When her first baby was born, Erin continued to work full time, but when a second daughter arrived three years later, she felt she had entered a new stage of life, one where attending to all her commitments—at home and on the job—would require some skill, sacrifice, and creativity.

Erin phoned her sister-in-law, Lacey, who worked as a human resources manager. Erin explained that she was racking her brain about how to continue to excel as a hospital administrator and a mother, now that she had two children under the age of five. Erin's mother had been the family's child-care provider, and that worked well initially. But Erin's full-time-plus hours left little time for her to spend with her children, and little time for Erin's mother to pursue her hobbies, take classes, or travel in her remaining years.

Lacey suggested Erin look into job sharing with another committed colleague who had the same skill set. "Do a little research and then make a proposal to your manager," Lacey advised. Erin did just that and within three months, she had set up a schedule whereby she worked three days one week and two days the next; her job-share partner worked the other days. She also had flexibility to work at home on some days.

The compromise? Erin had to take a step down on the career ladder and give up her management role, as the hospital wanted more consistency there. Erin didn't mind. In fact, she was a little relieved since her hectic home and work life was more than enough at the time. What she didn't want was to drop off top management's radar as an excellent, committed professional. She needn't have worried. The hospital knew that Erin—her talent, energy, and commitment—was an asset.

Today, Erin is again at a crossroads. She has one daughter in college, another in her last year of high school, her youngest entering eighth grade, and her boss is eager to put her back on track to become a top manager. Evidently, her decade away from the fast track did not harm her trajectory, it only slowed it down. She hasn't decided whether to get back on the fast track because, in her organization and industry, she knows that corner-office jobs come with demands for fifty- to sixty-hour workweeks and may not allow her to align her work-life priorities. Now approaching fifty, she wants to find synergy between her job, maintenance of her physical health, time with her husband and her last child at home, volunteering, and intellectual stimulation. She's also mindful that her own mother, who still helps the family during after-school hours, is aging.

Complicating factors even more, Erin's husband just left an enormously stressful job for a lower-paying post. The family could use the money (for many purposes, but especially college) that an executive job commands. And Erin is committed to the hospital that has stuck by her. Time, yet again, for Erin and her employer to think about the best way to create a different *custom fit*.

The Custom-Fit Workplace

This book is about more than rejecting long hours and unrealistic bosses before your family, friends, and you yourself slip away. It is about finding ways to create twenty-first-century work organizations that produce great results—so that businesses and their employees both thrive.

The Custom-Fit Workplace is not intellectual idealism or journalistic sensationalism. The people you will read about in these pages are real; they have been in the trenches, one way or another, figuring out new ways to work and how to build sustainable, prospering organizations and sane lives. They are pioneers blazing a new trail, putting ideas into practice, and helping us see a wealth of possibilities.[13]

One thing we have learned from our experiences of founding, working in, researching, and teaching about organizations is that leaders are everywhere, waiting to pick up the ball and run or to pick up the blocks and build something new. Some are chief executives of multinational companies, but others are accidental leaders: the boss who offered unlimited paid sick time to his two dozen employees as long as goals were met; the employee who needed a child-care solution so she started a drop-off center at her workplace. The people you will meet in these pages all tried working differently. They wanted to make their lives more manageable, productive, and real. In the process, they joined the ranks of people reinventing how we work. They didn't know they were pioneers. They just needed a custom fit.

We've written this book for managers and workers, salaried and hourly, in organizations of all types and sizes, including the union workforce. Overall, today's workplace isn't working for most people, yet the challenges keep growing. Change is needed. We present some proven options in this book that you may be able to implement or simply encourage others to try. Better still, you may have new ideas about how to create custom work arrangements that are efficient, effective, and sustainable over a life's changing course. We encourage you to take these ideas and use them to inspire other ways to build the *custom-fit workplace*. This is only the beginning of the journey. We invite you to join us.

Today's economic and workforce challenges have produced an extraordinary opportunity for people to step forward with new ways of working, building organizations, and creating value. No one has come up with *the* way to fit together the many pieces of the work-life puzzle. Maybe someday there will be a computer program that will take your personal data at a particular point in time and find you the perfect job: an "eJob/LifeHarmony" that makes the match. But until then, we offer the ideas in *The Custom-Fit Workplace* so that we all can celebrate both work and life.

2

THE CUSTOM-FIT WORKPLACE

Business Benefits

It seems like common sense. Trust your workers and treat them well, then watch them and your business thrive.

Common sense, yes, but where's the proof?

The proof is in the bottom line. We're not speaking figuratively; we're talking about the effect of custom-fit work practices on profitability. We understand that businesses face turnover they can't control, high absenteeism, skyrocketing medical costs, and a tough economy. The question likely on your mind is not whether or not custom-fit work arrangements make for great articles on the front page of the Business Section, but whether they make for good reading in the shareholders' report. If it's a number you want, let's start with this one: shareholder returns rose 3.5 percent in a Watson Wyatt study of the effects of flexible work practices.[1] But the true bottom-line benefit is more expansive, more complicated, and even more compelling.

A virtuous cycle forms when employers help employees have balanced lives and meet their responsibilities outside work. When employees are trusted and empowered to do their jobs, they work harder and give much more than the minimum. They are energized when they feel competent and see that they are appreciated and treated fairly. This energy translates into increased quantity and quality of output—and ultimately leads to improved productivity and profitability. The rewards do not stop there. That renewed energy also translates into worker commitment and loyalty, which reduces turnover and the cost of recruiting and training new employees. This improved employee performance and cost reduction boosts the company's financial performance.

Hundreds of business studies, from academic papers to internal corporate reports, can be piled from floor to ceiling (and in our homes, currently are) to show that without employee engagement and commitment, businesses are, at best, shaky. And hundreds of others show that giving workers custom-fit opportunities—choice in when, where, and how they work—is a spectacular motivation and engagement tool, an excellent means for cutting costs and reducing employee absence, and a tangible method for reaping the very real business benefits of employees' commitment and drive. The process through which a business's bottom line benefits from customized work arrangements includes attracting and recruiting talented employees, retaining committed workers and minimizing turnover costs, reducing absenteeism and overhead costs, and boosting quality and productivity. Custom fit equals good business.

U.S. INDUSTRY NEEDS NEW WORKPLACE PRACTICES

The traditional workplace structure leaches dollars from businesses every year. The by-products of a traditional structure—tardiness, absenteeism, and turnover, as well as workplace accidents—cost U.S. industry over $300 billion per year in lost productivity, health-care costs, and recruitment and retraining costs.[2]

Attract and Recruit Talented Workers

Every human resources manager and employer knows that good hiring is a challenge. It takes time, resources, and finesse. Poor hires are a costly affair that also affect the morale of everyone in the organization. Great hires, on the other hand, reward you with excellent productivity, ingenuity and drive, time saved in management and trouble-shooting, good team relationships, and longer-term employment. Great hiring starts with attracting and recruiting the best possible candidates. Contrary to what many managers believe, today the juiciest carrot to dangle for prospective employees is not cash—it's flexibility.

Dale, a semiretired dentist, told us that attracting the very best team to his office was one of the single most important determinants of a successful business. Using a team-based management philosophy, he accommodated parenting, school, and other needs to help him attract an array of talented, motivated workers. "Skills can be learned," he says. "Whether we're looking for dental assistants or front office staff, we look first and foremost for the very best people, regardless of previous experience. When necessary, we then train them to suit the job." As a small business owner in a small city with little ability to flash around cash and bonuses like a big tech or financial firm, he was rewarded nonetheless by employees who were happy, productive, and willing to go above and beyond the call of duty to take care of clients. Turnover was nearly nonexistent, and people spent ten, twenty, even thirty years in his employ. Dale's intuition is buoyed by research. Compensation consultants The Hay Group reported in an annual study that employees today actively seek employers whose values fit with their own.[3] Additionally, a study of hourly workers in a large U.S. retail store credits offering flexibility around scheduling as a key to the firm's status as a "premium employer" and therefore a great way to recruit top talent.[4]

Countless studies show that employee-friendly policies that accommodate work-life needs have an enhanced ability to attract and recruit the best people, whether to family-owned businesses or to tech giants. Fully two-thirds of human resources managers surveyed said supportive, employer-friendly policies are the most important factor in attracting and retaining employees, and nearly one in three U.S. workers say that being able to flexibly balance work and life is the most important factor in considering job offers.[5]

In the ever more competitive global business environment, building a bigger, better, and more diverse talent pool from which to draw potential employees simply makes good business sense. The ages, skills, and life stages of the men and women seeking new work arrangements are diverse. Gen Ys approach the workplace expecting a degree of flexibility, and 85 percent of under-thirties report they want more of it. Move up the age scale a few decades, and you find highly coveted, experienced, knowledgeable workers looking for phased retirement. This group, too, is especially apt to seek out flexible workplaces. The New Retirement Survey shows that Baby Boomer women, especially, see retirement not as stagnant golden years but instead as an opportunity for career development.

Women like Anita and Erin, introduced in Chapter One, are eager to find ways to maneuver to meet the competing demands of their lives. So are most women, from hourly retail workers to the Canadian women executives at the top of their game who prioritized a balance between work and life as an 8.5 rating on a scale of 10 in evaluating potential employers.[6] But it's not just mothers or even just women in general who find flexibility attractive. Men do, too. In a 2005 survey of Fortune 500 male senior executives, 84 percent reported the desire to integrate work and life, with 55 percent willing to forgo income for it. In a study of two-career couples, more than half of the men wanted an option to customize their career path by slowing down from the fast track when family demands became pressing and ramping back up when those demands diminished later in life.[7]

The case of Carlos, a highly sought-after candidate when he graduated from law school six years ago, shows what all these numbers mean in practice. He received offers from his two top firms of choice—call them Firm A and Firm B. Both touted a great and dynamic staff and interesting practice areas. Ultimately, his decision came down to one thing: expectation for billable hours. While some of his classmates chose Firm A, which offered the higher salary, Carlos knew he wanted an employer that marketed itself as a lifestyle firm; he had visions of taking off early on winter Fridays to hit the slopes, and taking full advantage of a generous paternity leave policy someday. So he traded the higher salary for the flexibility that came with Firm B and an ability to forge his own custom fit. As more and more recruits like Carlos seek more out of life than a paycheck, custom fit gives smart businesses the edge.

Attracting the best and the brightest with flexible policies and working with each employee to find a custom fit rewards the company immediately in terms of worker productivity and engagement. And great hires go beyond immediate good fits to become good-fits-that-last, minimizing the loss of institutional knowledge and training investments, turnover costs, and the attendant price paid in morale that high turnover brings.

Retain Committed Workers

In early 2010, with one in ten Americans unemployed, The Conference Board, a business information organization, found those who still had jobs were far from uniformly grateful; many were less happy than ever before. In fact, of the five thousand U.S. households surveyed, only 45 percent were satisfied with their jobs, with those under twenty-five topping the dissatisfied list, and Baby Boomers not far behind. Two decades ago, 60 percent of the Boomer generation whistled as they worked. Now, only 46 percent do. Perhaps most striking, nearly a quarter of the survey respondents overall didn't expect to be in the same job a year hence, numbers that The Conference Board says should raise a big red flag.[8] These are numbers that are not tied to the current bad economy; they show a continuing downward trend in employee satisfaction.

Even with so many people eager to fill open jobs, it pays for employers to stanch the bleeding of the workers they have. It was startling to us that so few managers we spoke with seemed to understand that beyond morale issues and time, turnover is extremely expensive, costing a company about 150 percent of a salaried employee's yearly pay to bring in a replacement, and 50–75 percent of an hourly worker's yearly pay. Turnover is a major consideration for businesses that want to remain competitive, and was a serious enough problem for Deloitte & Touche that, when the company slowed the exodus, the estimated savings were $41.5 million.

To keep the workers and save the millions, Deloitte & Touche didn't resort to drastic measures like bolting the doors or bribing workers with promises of trips to Tahiti. What it did was to redesign the career track (a custom-fit technique covered in Chapter Five), so it could retain valuable employees and increase the odds of their returning after time off. Deloitte's choice was bolstered not only by these potential cost savings but also by research. According to a recent Met-Life Survey, achieving work-life fit is second only to on-the-job relationships in determining if a person stays with an employer.[9] The Conference Board found that 80 percent of one large firm's workforce said being able to balance work and home affected their career choice and their desire to stay with the company.[10] And one study of 614 businesses demonstrated that flexibility outranked above-market salaries, stock options, and training as a factor in retaining workers.[11] Scores of businesses, from retailers to manufacturers to insurance companies, have found that the way to recreate the loyal career employee of the past is to offer one or more of the work arrangements described in this book and show respect and consideration in management.

Some of the best-known companies in the United States recognize the promise inherent in this reciprocity, and have used work-from-home options, alternative schedules, part-time employment, and job shares to slash turnover. Fortune 500 financial services company USAA increased its net worth and paid out $857 million in dividends and other distributions in 2008, a year rocked by the implosion of financial institutions. It also cut its turnover rate in half by instituting a compressed workweek, allowing employees to work full time with an alternative schedule.[12] Wholesale retailer Costco, which employs both union and non-union employees, boasts a turnover rate that is one-third of the industry average, and cites flexibility and efforts to give part-time employees predictability as key reasons it retains its employees better than rival Sam's Club.[13] Managers at companies including Amway, Bristol-Meyers Squibb, Honeywell, Kraft, Lucent Technologies, and Motorola reported that telecommuting and flexible work options enhanced retention.[14] From the five hundred managers and professionals retained at Cigna to the 50 percent reduction in turnover for Corning's manufacturing workers, flexibility and respect for worker responsibilities outside of work clearly builds loyalty and worker satisfaction able to withstand other market pressures.[15]

Though dedicated, productive workers who stay on for decades are every employer's dream, even retaining employees in the short term helps the bottom line. Employees with access to flexible work arrangements are less likely to leave their current employers for at least a year.[16] Low-wage workers, often employed in high-turnover sectors, were found to be 30 percent less likely to leave their employer within two years if they had flexibility than workers who had none.[17] Even a little flexibility goes a long way. Retail workers allowed to deviate from the customary working hours of 8 AM to 4 PM or 2 PM to 10 PM were more loyal and committed to their employers, boosting retention.[18]

MOTHERS DON'T OPT OUT OF A GOOD FIT

Pressures caused by changes like having a baby can trigger an employee's departure. Alternative work arrangements can help businesses keep those they have trained and invested in. Women are more likely to stay with an employer after having a child when they feel their employer is responsive to their work-family needs and are more likely to return to the same employer after giving birth when businesses accommodate work-life pressures.[19]

When an employer is supportive of work-life integration needs, employees give back to the business through increased loyalty (that is, they stay put). The cost savings attributed to reduced turnover are just the beginning. Flexibility and the mutual respect it represents changes the fundamental relationship between workers and their employers for improved client relationships and enhanced financial performance, too.

Engage, Motivate, and Unleash Worker Performance

People with some control over when, where, and how they work are more satisfied, engaged, and committed to their employers. These "warm and fuzzy" intangibles—feelings, perceptions, responses—drive them to work hard and stay motivated and productive. Many studies, in fact, document how employee-friendly, customized work arrangements promote job satisfaction and employee engagement, creativity, and motivation—all of which directly impact a range of business performance outcomes from quality of product or service to market share.

HAPPY WORKERS EQUAL HAPPY BOTTOM LINE

A study of 5,500 employees in one hundred organizations found a direct correlation between worker satisfaction and a firm's profitability, while another found companies with highly committed employees had a 112 percent return to shareholders over three years, compared to only 90 percent for those with average commitment and only 76 percent for companies with workers expressing a low degree of commitment.[20]

According to research at Workplace Flexibility 2010, an institute at Georgetown University, workers with access to flexible work schedules appear more willing to work hard to help their employers succeed.[21] Further, numerous studies show that employees are likely to give extra effort—what's called "discretionary voluntary behavior," such as making improvements, attending nonrequired meetings, and assisting others with job duties—when the work-life benefits offered by their employers are perceived to be useful.[22] Really, the cause and effect is quite simple, and we've all either experienced it in our own workplace or observed it as a customer. Employee satisfaction correlates directly to customer retention and satisfaction—or, as one manager says, "If your employees are happy, they'll take care of your customers."[23]

Not only does satisfaction correlate to work with a smile, research shows it means more work and better work, too. When people are satisfied with their jobs and feel cared for, they are more motivated and more productive, whether they work in low-wage hourly jobs or high-wage jobs in a Fortune 500 company. Corporate Voices for Working Families found that the engagement level of low-wage workers was 50 percent higher for those with flexibility and that these workers were more likely to feel they had a stake in their organization.[24] Hourly workers in a large U.S. retail store who were able to work the hours they preferred (to allow them better fit with their off-the-job commitments) were happier, less distracted, had more energy and better attitudes, and were excited about where they worked. Like the manager quoted earlier, their managers reported a clear connection between their customized schedules and job performance metrics such as customer service, sales, and profits.[25]

Customization and flexibility in the workplace improve the work and attitudes of professional workers as well, workers whose commitment doesn't necessarily come standard with a big paycheck. The authors of *Womenomics* found that blue chip companies (including KPMG, Microsoft, and Pfizer) offering some customization of hours were more competitive, productive, and inhabited by less stressed and more loyal employees than were those that did not.[26] Loyalty or commitment for workers overall regularly translates to productivity and a higher level of performance: for example, a Corporate Leadership Council study concluded that every 10 percent improvement in employee commitment increases that person's discretionary effort by 6 percent and performance by 2 percent.[27]

Using a team or results-based approach can also improve the bottom line of companies willing to commit to these fundamental shifts in business philosophy. Scholars Huselid and Becker studied hundreds of companies of different sizes across industries, and found that high-performance work practices (such as those described in Chapter Nine) increase productivity and reduce turnover, thereby leading to increased market share and profits. They found that the strongest improvements in market performance come from businesses that go beyond lip service and actually treat their workforce as a strategic asset rather than a cost to be minimized.[28]

Overall, what many of us feel in our gut—treat people well and they'll go above and beyond—turns out to be backed up by the numbers. Employee-friendly, customized work options promote job satisfaction and commitment, employee engagement, creativity, and motivation, which in turn lead to better performance outcomes such as quality, productivity, innovation, and market share.[29] There's nothing fuzzy about that.

Reduce Absenteeism and Overhead Costs

Custom-fit solutions like flexible hours and virtual work lead to clear savings in reduced absenteeism and overhead. Even if employees don't go so far as to leave their jobs because they can't make work and life mesh, without alternative work options their health can suffer and absenteeism can skyrocket due to illness or scheduling conflicts. The costs are significant: absenteeism can cost large employers more than a million dollars each year.[30] Companies that offer flexibility, by contrast, see absenteeism fall and cost savings mount. When employees have the ability to customize their schedules, they are more able to schedule appointments outside work hours and make up work, if needed, so they can deal with unexpected obligations. In one study, 63 percent of workers utilizing flexible work arrangements credited them as the reason for being absent less often.[31] Similarly, using a team-based approach to flexible scheduling, Chubb Insurance reduced unscheduled absences by 50 percent each month and overtime by 40 percent per employee.[32]

Allowing workers flexibility in where they work, in addition to when, also slashes costs related to absenteeism, as well as real estate and overhead. The Sloan Work and Family Research Network reports that telecommuting cuts absenteeism by nearly 60 percent.[33] Not only does virtual work keep people on the job, but as a flexibility strategy it can be extremely advantageous for companies facing real estate pressures and rising overhead costs. Corporations including IBM, AT&T, Sun Microsystems, JetBlue, ARO, and Holland America have saved millions in real estate and other expenses with telecommuting, an issue covered in depth in Chapter Four.

Taken collectively, the research and case studies demonstrate the financial gains offered by custom and flexible work arrangements. Some of the cost savings are direct—such as being able to eliminate buildings or an entire campus by turning a team virtual—while other savings are realized as the result of happier, healthier employees who don't feel they must choose between either work or life and family. Either way, it is clear that the better balance sheet belongs to the flexible, custom-fit workplace.

Other Benefits: Healthier Employees, Families, and Communities

Not all the benefits of custom work arrangements and employee-friendly work practices accrue to the business, of course. Employees, their families, and their communities also benefit. Studies show that workers with flexible work arrangements reap a multitude of personal benefits. They exhibit less stress and burnout, they sleep more, and they are better able to relax and unwind.[34] They have more energy and healthier lifestyles.[35] Their mental health is better than that of other workers, and this is even truer for low-income workers.[36] A 2009 report by the Work, Family and Health Network compiled evidence that employers' policies can directly impact workers' risk of cardiovascular disease and thus add years to a person's life—or subtract them![37] The Work and Family Institute's 2009 report, The State of Health in the American Workforce, concurs: too many workers are stressed-out and time-strapped and the result is a U.S. workforce where just 28 percent say they are in excellent health (down from 34 percent six years ago). The findings are "a wake-up call for employers and employees alike to take a closer look at how their organizations affect people's health and well-being," says Ellen Galinsky, director of the institute.[38]

Work customization can help improve the health of employees' families too. One recent study linked parental work-life conflict with childhood obesity; it called for flexible work schedules to allow employees to sit down regularly with children for dinner at home and take them to the doctor regularly.[39] Another study found that family leave policies reduce childhood mortality during the time periods parents spend with children (that they otherwise would not be able to spend) because they are on leave.[40]

Work customization might also contribute to a greener environment. Although there's no hard data yet, we believe that virtual work—by reducing the number of workers who commute to work every day—certainly helps. Everyone who's ever experienced a long commute can also attest to the psychological benefits of avoiding the stress of being stuck in commuter traffic. Cases in point: Citigroup's "Alternative Workplace Strategies" initiative was launched in 2006 to cut energy consumption 15 percent via office sharing and remote work.[41] And the city of Houston launched a "flex in the city" two-week program to encourage all companies to allow telecommuting and flexible working hours to keep the air cleaner and do their part to reduce greenhouse gas emissions.[42] It was so successful at slashing worker stress, easing notoriously congested commutes, and boosting worker productivity that the city vowed to repeat it every year.

BUSINESS AND PEOPLE BENEFIT FROM CUSTOMIZED BENEFITS

In a fascinating study of 527 businesses, scholars Perry-Smith and Blum examined the effect of offering customizable clusters of policies to help employees integrate work and life priorities.[43] The policies included, among other options, customized leaves, on-site child care, and flexible scheduling. What Perry-Smith and Blum found was that performance was higher in firms where the benefits could be "clustered" for an individualized fit. Being willing to invest in employees by connecting them with their families and their families to the business represents, the authors argued, a "fundamental paradigm shift" toward greater trust in the workplace.

Case Closed

People are your most important asset. Hundreds of business books and articles reach this conclusion, yet not enough businesses have internalized the message, regardless of how many of them repeat it. Even more studies show how businesses can thrive by unleashing the creativity, commitment, and loyalty of employees. Customized, employee-friendly, flexible work arrangements help businesses do just that. Yes, employees need and want them, but businesses and their shareholders benefit as much or more when employees have access to and are encouraged to avail themselves of these arrangements and policies. The case for such workplace practices is so strong that in 2005 Corporate Voices for Working Families called for an end to the debate about the utility of work-life initiatives! What is needed now is not another study but a culture shift that encourages people and businesses to implement existing custom work arrangements and develop new ones.

3

FLEXIBILITY AT WORK

The Basics of Custom Fit

Embarking on a journey toward changing the American work-place, it's wise to remember that every journey begins with a single step. Denver businessman Jim Johnson took that step several years ago when he attended a talk by law professor Joan Williams, director of the Center for WorkLife Law. Jim's wife, herself an attorney frustrated by how her work and personal life were too often at odds, convinced him to go. Moved by both the logic of Williams's arguments and the moral urgency to make work compatible with family responsibilities, Jim decided to reorganize his hundred-year-old company. Johnson Moving & Storage now offers flexible options to approximately 30 percent of its 225 employees, including customer-service representatives, order-entry people, and long-distance dispatchers.[1] Jim spells out the results: turnover nearly eliminated; gross profit above the industry average; quality rank of number one in seven of nine markets; less wage pressure; winner of industry awards—not to mention excellent press in outlets ranging from CNN to the *New York Times*.

Consider this chapter step one on *your* journey, whether you are a worker who would welcome a custom fit, a manager looking to improve productivity, or CEO intent upon retaining key employees and boosting profits. Building a custom fit depends upon the successful integration of work and life, and flexible policies in the workplace are the building blocks that allow each employee and company to create a configuration that works. This all starts with the basic flexible arrangements already successfully used by companies like Jim's: variations of alternative scheduling, reduced workload, and virtual work. The good news is that many workplaces—as of 2008, more than half of all U.S. companies—report using at least one of these strategies in some way. You probably already know someone who takes advantage of such an option: a nurse who works four ten-hour shifts each week, an administrator who negotiated a thirty-two-hour reduced schedule, or a sales rep who works from a home office when not on the road. These common flexible work arrangements affect when, how, and where people work, and are critical pieces of the custom-fit workplace.

Though half of all companies may have already adopted one or more of these options—in theory or perhaps even in print as company policy—that unfortunately doesn't mean the practices are actually being used, or used successfully. To make flexible work benefit companies and workers alike in the real business world, it will be necessary to begin to close this gap between policy and practice.

Alternative Scheduling

The freedom to choose when to work takes myriad forms—from the data-entry specialist who prefers early morning hours when the office is quiet and production is easiest to the city planner who works four long days but takes Fridays off to teach karate. As discussed in Chapter Two, alternative scheduling options including flexible hours and compressed workweeks are one way to help improve work-life integration for everyone, boost productivity and commitment, and lower costs associated with turnover and absenteeism.

Flexible Hours

One of the simplest ways to introduce flexibility into the workplace, a flexible hours arrangement allows each employee to customize starting and quitting times, while remaining present during "core" times as needed—to accommodate a standing meeting, or to ensure maximum coverage for specific hours of each day known to be busier than others. Employees usually negotiate flexible hours arrangements individually with employers based on need or desire, making it incumbent upon the manager to stay open to the change in the absence of company policy to guide the decision. Managers inclined to reject the notion out of hand might consider the main reasons employees are consistently late or burned out: long commutes or traffic snarls, kids' school schedules, or poor health, to name a few. Instead of reacting to the end results (tardy or absent employees), why not set employees up for success and reduce your own workload on the back end?

As an example, April works as a logistics specialist for an online jewelry retailer. She is also a passionate yoga practitioner whose favorite yoga class starts at 3:30 PM. April arranged with her boss to start work very early each day (6 AM), and though she departs early in the afternoon (2:30), she's on duty when important deliveries need to go out. She is grateful to her boss for the flexibility, and has dismissed other job leads because she doubts she'd get so much control over her schedule anywhere else. Yoga helps April keep a healthy, balanced life, and she feels she is a better worker for it. Her employer, while expending no money and little effort, benefits from April's improved energy and overall good health, and has also avoided losing April to a competitor by considering and accommodating her needs.

April's hours may be extreme, but even small adjustments in a worker's schedule can solve real problems. If Marta can work ten to six instead of nine to five, she is able to shave an hour and a half off her commute, saving her substantial money each month and allowing her time to head up her Women in Banking business group that meets in the early mornings. If Bennet can drop his daughter off at day care and be at work at 9:00 instead of 8:30, he avoids additional child-care costs and enjoys a morning ritual special to them both. He then works later in the day while his wife picks their daughter up. The impact such minor changes can have on workers' lives is substantial, as they have more control, more time for family and friends, and maybe even more time for themselves.

Flexible hours may also involve taking off larger chunks of time, following a project-based schedule. Angel, a salaried designer who works all night to meet a Wednesday deadline, might take Thursday off to relax. In this case, the arrangement Angel has with his employer is for him to take the time it takes to get the work done, and then be rewarded for it with unquestioned comp time. His employer is treating him as a competent professional and giving him ownership of the work; in turn, he is motivated to both get the work done and make sure he gets the rejuvenation he needs in the aftermath. Compare this to a traditional model, in which Angel would burn the midnight oil to meet his deadline as part of his job, and be expected bright and early the next morning to get started on another project. It's fair to say the traditional model might get him there in body the next workday, but certainly not in spirit.

In fact, there is no downside to flexible hours, so long as the benefit is used respectfully by all. A worker can't let a 10 AM start time slip to 10:30 without making prior arrangements. And an employer shouldn't use the option as a way to avoid paying overtime. An hourly employee who is consistently working ten-hour shifts and then told to take the extra hours off the following week is not so much being treated as a professional as being cheated out of overtime pay. Leslie, the assistant manager of a health clinic, was presented with a new alleged flextime benefit that meant that extra time spent in one day could be taken off within the week. Yet in reality, job demands (and her manager) never allowed that to happen, with the result that she was overworked *and* being cheated out of overtime pay.

Flexible-hours arrangements require trust and open communication between employee and employer. When this trust exists, it signals a heightened plane of respect and dignity each party brings to the work at hand. Here's how to make flexible hours work:

- Don't underestimate the power of changing one person's schedule even in small increments in either direction. Minute changes can add up to important shifts in people's lives.
- Employees and employers should work together to create schedules that work for company and personal needs. Don't stick to rigid scheduling simply out of tradition.
- If you're making a case for a flexible schedule to management, cite the business benefits of worker loyalty, decreased absenteeism, and even improved health.

Flexible hours are a basic custom-fit strategy, one that can drastically reduce stress and overload in people's lives and contribute greatly to job satisfaction and productivity at work.

Compressed Workweeks

Another common form of alternative scheduling, compressed workweeks alter the traditional nine-to-five schedule in a set pattern without reducing total working hours or full-time income. In a compressed workweek, hours can be arranged in a multitude of ways, from the most common 4/40 (four ten-hour days with one free day within each week), to an arrangement called 5–4/9 or 9/80, whereby a worker is scheduled for a week of five nine-hour days followed by a week of four nine-hour days, allowing for one day off every other week.

In some fields, such as health care, compressed workweeks are already fairly standard. Overall, 39 percent of businesses sampled in the 2005 National Study of Employers allowed some workers this type of schedule, while 10 percent made this flexible arrangement available to most or all of their employees.

For many people, having one weekday free is enormously helpful. It provides time to exercise, pursue a hobby, volunteer, or schedule dental appointments and parent-teacher meetings. Other positive outcomes of this arrangement include nonstandard commute times because of extended-day schedules and the preservation of full-time pay and benefits. As it happens, having a free day can also make a substantive difference in stress and absenteeism, which benefits employer and employee alike. An employee who needs to run a mundane errand like renewing a driver's license during standard working hours can plan to do so on the free day instead of leaving work to deal with the chore.

Compressed work schedules do have a downside to workers. On a day-to-day level, free time is reduced by those longer shifts, so a person is less available for responsibilities and recreation outside work. And not every person or every job is a good fit for the physical and mental intensity of longer shifts. For some, finding regular care for children or older family members who need help can be made more challenging because of the longer daily schedule.

Management may also be challenged by a compressed work arrangement. It can be tricky to ensure adequate supervision during extended hours. For certain types of businesses, it may take some adjustment to arrange operational coverage on an employee's off-day. Managers also need to keep an eye out for decreased productivity from stress and fatigue.

Challenges need not be barriers, however, and research shows that motivated employers and workers who choose these alternatives find ways to surmount the obstacles. That was the case when Raytheon Missile Systems implemented 9/80 work schedules.

Raytheon's president, Louise Francesconi, initiated a program in 1997 to boost recruitment and retention of key employees. Working nine-hour days with every other Friday off became the new norm for salaried workers. In order to allay fears and make sure the program launched successfully, the company formed a cross-functional team to research and strategize ways to overcome challenges across departments. According to Raytheon's management, absenteeism dropped and productivity increased, as did employee willingness to pitch in for overtime when needed. Employees love the Fridays off and the program has been a good selling point for new recruits. These are the main keys to Raytheon's success:

- Being flexible (about flexibility). Though this is the customary work schedule, managers are allowed to adjust it to fit the needs of individual employees. Some opted to retain their standard forty hours a week, or elected to work half-days on all Fridays.
- Rolling out the program to all of Raytheon's salaried employees at once established a feeling of "culture change" and also allowed the integration of differing schedules and ability to cover all positions as necessary.

Eight thousand of Raytheon's eleven thousand employees currently use this work schedule.[2] According to Raytheon WorkLife & Wellness Manager Anne Palmer, employees have become protective of the 9/80 schedule. "When we had a new president come on board last year, the biggest, most often asked question was 'You're not going to take the 9/80 away are you?' And she has to reiterate that still today because it is so popular." It's become the new norm for Anne as well, who says that "after all these years, I can't imagine not working this schedule! *Love* flexibility."[3]

Reduced Workload

Another option, for those who can afford it, is to reduce the workload by switching to a part-time schedule, or job sharing.[4] Reducing workload allows people who are financially able to lower their pay and benefits in exchange for increased flexibility and less time at work. It includes such common options as part-time jobs and job sharing. Women, especially, take advantage of this opportunity, making up 70 percent of the part-time workforce. While some employees have reduced workloads because of company-dictated cost-cutting measures, research shows that 68 percent of women and 51 percent of men who do so *choose* a reduced workload.[5] Various best practices maximize the benefits and address the challenges of part-time work, and job sharing is increasingly popular as a way to make two part-time workers and their employer reap the benefits of custom fit.

Part-Time, for Real

Part-time work is one of the most common custom-fit solutions, but it's often greeted with uncertainty by employee and employer alike. Employees, especially full-time or salaried workers, may fear their workload won't decrease commensurate with their pay or that they won't be considered dedicated and they'll be passed over for promotions or bonuses. Employers and managers may fear that they'll be left holding the bag or working extra to compensate for part-timers, that communication will suffer, that additional hires will increase overhead costs, or that client needs won't be met quickly enough, damaging the company's reputation.

These are all credible concerns, but with attention to the following guidelines, both sides have a better chance for a successful arrangement:

- Reduced hours ideally equal a reduced workload.
- An employee who is working, say, 80 percent time should be compensated 80 percent of a full-time salary, not less.
- Part-time work should be treated without stigma from colleagues and employers, or else risk the employee's disengagement.

- Both managers and employees need to take initiative in ensuring communication is clear so that no information falls through the cracks.
- Benefits must be addressed in a manner that is fair for both the employee and the company.
- Both employee and employer need to ensure that the work is completed successfully, whether that work is responding to a client or finishing a project on deadline.

For companies, part-time arrangements may make it necessary to be more creative, and to weigh the investment in finding a solution and any additional costs with the retention of the employee. Accommodating part-time workers may make it necessary to hire and manage more people. However, those additional people bring potential benefits. In a crunch or to cover an absence there are more people who are trained and ready to go. Employees waiting in the wings can be trained and developed to cover the part-time worker's job, allowing for coverage and bringing out the best in a latent worker. Because of the heightened commitment created by a company's efforts to accommodate employees' needs, it will have a deeper, more loyal, pool of human resources to draw from.

It is worth noting as well that oftentimes part-time arrangements are only temporary. Understanding and accommodating a part-time work request means an employer will not only experience positives such as less stress and absenteeism on the part of the worker, it may just keep brain drain at bay—keeping that highly skilled and experienced worker from taking those assets elsewhere. It pays to work to accommodate a part-time request; in the likely event the employee returns to a full-time schedule, the employer will be further rewarded for the accommodation by retaining a loyal employee with good institutional knowledge.

Certain jobs, like health-care work, are very suitable for part-time arrangements, whereas other jobs, perhaps those that require tight teamwork or management of a large group of employees, may not seem so at first glance. We would argue that most jobs, the presidency perhaps excepted (though a job share might provide relief or built-in bipartisanship), are worth a thorough investigation before rejecting the idea outright.

When Kelly, a mid-level manager at a creative agency, asked if she could take Thursdays off, her employer balked. Her boss felt she was drowning under the work she already had, and didn't see a way to give that work to anyone else. Was Kelly's job truly not amenable to part-time work, or was the option summarily dismissed because Kelly's job had not been done on a part-time basis before? Could Kelly have trained or mentored someone on her team to help cover her responsibilities? Would a job-share arrangement have solved the problem? Or perhaps arranging for reduced hours in the office and follow-up at home might have worked. With some creativity and flexible thinking, even jobs that don't at first seem conducive to part-time arrangements can be configured for a win-win, if both parties see the advantages in making it work.

Case in point, the legal field is not known for being part-time friendly, but Cindy, an associate for a midsized law firm, has made inroads by being deliberate in what she wants, flexible about the terms, and innovative in her strategies. She'd already worked for her firm for several years when she had her first child. She proposed that she work half-time, but that she retain paid benefits and receive a bonus that was being awarded to all associates that year. At the time, the firm was experiencing a high attrition rate and Cindy was a good performer, so they agreed to her requests. Within six months, Cindy had bumped up her workload to 60 percent. She has maintained that level through having another child, and anticipates resuming her full workload once both children are in school.

A creative compensation system helps the arrangement work. Cindy gets the same amount of pay each pay period, but she also keeps money in a reserve account at the firm. If her hours fall under 60 percent, the firm pulls money from it; if her hours go *over* 60 percent, which is usually the case, the firm gives her a bonus check for that pay period. In this way, both the firm and Cindy are treated fairly.

Flexible hours also make this part-time arrangement work. Cindy's husband has a variable schedule, and as a result, Cindy's hours fluctuate from week to week. Her firm allows her this freedom, asking only that she always work full days on Wednesdays, and that she be available at certain hours each day. As a result, clients never have to wait too long before hearing back from her, and she's available daily to partners who may need her.

One of the challenges of part-time work is the issue of benefits. Unlike Cindy's firm, many employers are not able or willing to pay full benefits for a part-time employee, and yet those costs are daunting for an employee to bear alone. Generally, those who take a part-time job and get benefits understand that the benefits are a significant aspect of their compensation, and are more willing to accept a lower salary as a result. Typically, benefits and salary must be rolled into one and considered as a whole. It becomes part of the negotiation. Pam, a librarian, works half-time, and pays for half of her benefits. The county that employs her pays for the other half. The arrangement works well and feels fair to both parties, which is critical to the success of part-time work.

Job Shares

A clever variation on the part-time option is the job share, a resourceful solution that leaves no duties or clients untended. Job sharing creates flexibility for two employees who divide the duties of one position in exchange for complementary schedules and part-time pay. There is a great degree of customization with job-sharing arrangements, as the division of labor will depend greatly upon the position, the field, and the skill sets of the people involved. And not everyone is well-suited to sharing a job and possesses the discipline and rigorous communication required for success.

Finding the right job-share partner, a task usually left to the person requesting the change, is "a little like dating," according to Jennifer Turano, whose experiences sharing an advertising sales job at *Glamour* magazine appeared in the *New York Times*.[6] Just as with romance, "you can sense right away whether there's a connection." And Turano took her time to find "the one" after she applied for her position as a job share and had her first prospective job partner back out at the last minute. Turano persevered, making it easy for her potential employer to say yes. "I told the manager who interviewed me that I still wanted to work at *Glamour*, and that if she hired me, I'd be responsible for all the accounts myself until I could find another partner. I was determined to do everything possible to make job-sharing a success."

Turano's experience is borne out by data that suggest many of the myths surrounding job shares, such as the fear that they require more coordination and supervision on the part of the manager, are just that—myths. Because the responsibility to make the arrangement work rests primarily with the employees, they appear to make a concerted effort to maintain top performance without burdening their managers. Turano and her partner, Joan O'Rourke, share about twenty accounts, most of which are large companies, and both know every detail about each client. They take pains to make the arrangement easy for others, including sharing a phone number and e-mail address to streamline communication. The women also recognize another sticking point for some companies when it comes to job-shares: though the two divide their commissions, they both receive full benefits, representing an increase in costs for the magazine. Yet it's all part of the benefit, salary, and value package both sides need to unwrap. Because Turano and O'Rourke recognize they are an expensive team, they have additional incentive to be high-performing. And they deliver. The two—referred to at *Glamour* as one person, "Jen and Joan"—won salesperson of the year in 2008.[7]

In order to support job shares and make this a viable flexible option, organizations are encouraged to develop written policies with clear guidelines—such as how pay will be prorated, benefits, communication expectations, and goals. It's equally critical for management to demonstrate support for the policy and stay committed. TAP Pharmaceuticals, which implemented a job-sharing program for its field sales employees in order to retain key employees who were starting families, advises that getting a program like this off the ground isn't simple. "You really need management buy-in, guidelines, and the company needs to invest in the effort. It can take years to establish a successful program."[8]

If you're looking at this option for your job, you need to first ask yourself if you have the right skills and desire to make it work. In addition to making a strong and clear business case when asking or applying for a job share, business writer Eve Nicholas has the following tips:

- Take the burden off your employer by finding a partner who will divide the workload and benefits with you. Compatible goals and qualities and complementary expertise and skills hold great importance.

- Present a combined résumé and proposal. Ideally, job-share partners should have shared expertise but different strengths to make the case even more compelling. Write a proposal that breaks down the details of your agreement, such as the hours you will each work, your respective responsibilities, and a plan for seamless communication. Make a strong business case, including how any costs might be offset by savings.[9]

Part-time work is a flexible work arrangement that permits a custom fit for many people. It helps people keep their job and professional skills sharp during phases of life when outside responsibilities may preclude full-time work—in this way, it helps workers maintain their economic security. Part-time work allows businesses to retain employees—and their expertise and value added—when they cannot work full-time hours. It's a win-win. When part-time arrangements work, everyone is happy.

Virtual Work

Telecommuting, working remotely, work-from-home, virtual work—these are all terms that describe using technology to perform part or all of your work from a remote location. Chapter Four goes into virtual work more extensively, but it is so useful for creating a custom fit that it also merits discussion here.

A schedule divided between the workplace and home or another remote location can allow the best of both worlds for workers looking for flexibility in start and end times—people who need to take care of an aging parent, are taking classes, have recurrent doctors' appointments, need to pick up kids from school, or work another job. For too many of us, checking e-mail at home or on our smart phones is simply an unwritten expectation that is not recognized as part of our workday—or, ironically, available as a flexible work option. One manager we spoke to said it simply wasn't possible for one of his employees to work from home on Fridays because the employee himself was also a manager, requiring his in-office presence in order to be effective. Never mind that the employee was wasting up to three hours in his Friday commute because of additional weekend traffic; never mind that the employee routinely worked remotely on weekends and in the evenings; never mind that the manager who shared this story was at the time working remotely.

Though it can be hard to step outside entrenched work patterns, formalizing remote work can help ameliorate this ever-extending workday and surprise employees and employers alike with how much gets done. Research shows that far more people can do their jobs effectively out of the office than is commonly assumed. Research from the Employment Policy Foundation suggests 65 percent of jobs could be done remotely, yet less than 30 percent of managers and professionals work virtually even one day a week, and far fewer in more blue-collar jobs.[10]

Interestingly, according to a December 2008 report from the U.S. Office of Personnel Management, 60 percent of federal agencies included virtual work in their emergency and continuity of operations plans in 2007, yet only 7 percent of eligible federal employees regularly use it.[11] Does it really take an H1N1 scare to make virtual work a real option? As will be discussed in Chapter Four, virtual work is a richly customizable opportunity, one that allows workers to more readily define on-the-clock hours and free time, spend less or no time commuting, and work at optimum hours, all while maximizing productivity and minimizing interruptions. As with all custom work arrangements, top-to-bottom management support and policies are key ingredients for virtual work to succeed.

Flexibility for Hourly Workers

While the flexible work arrangements covered thus far are some of the most common in use today, they are more frequently used by and available to professional and salaried workers.[12] Often neglected in discussions (and books) about work-life fit are hourly workers, especially those with low pay, who typically have less access to flexibility options.[13] That hourly workers are often unionized adds yet another dimension to forging a custom fit by introducing another voice into the conversation, one we explore in depth in Chapter Eight.

The truth is that hourly workers need flexibility possibly more than their professional counterparts. A full 25 percent of parents care for their children by working different shifts rather than putting them in child care, making predictable work schedules and flexible options a necessity.[14] The cost of child care is too great for some families, making "tag team" working and parenting the only viable option for them.

Although some mistakenly assume that hourly workers have, by definition, a flexible schedule (since they can presumably work as few as ten hours a week, or as many as forty or more), that is not the case. A 2006 Labor Project for Working Families study found two-thirds of people making over $71,000 a year had some ability to flex their schedules, while less than one-third of those earning less than $28,000 a year could do so.[15] While some companies offer flexible options to their entire workforce, many do not, failing to recognize that high turnover and absenteeism is a real cost they could substantially reduce by extending flexibility to those who need to be physically present, either in a retail environment, service job, or on a manufacturing line.

Many employers fail to offer hourly employees flexibility in their schedules precisely because they cut costs by adapting their staffing needs to the business cycle. To fit the business's needs, according to University of Chicago School of Social Service Administration professor Susan Lambert, a current trend in retail is a new status called "full-time flex" in which employees' time and pay "flexes" between 32 and 40 hours a week, *at the discretion of management*. These hourly workers have poor job stability and, not surprisingly, high levels of absenteeism and turnover—as high as 79 percent for some retailers.[16]

Research shows that the effort involved in offering appropriate flexible work options to hourly workers is worth it and can create a stable and loyal workforce that makes management far easier. It also involves a careful algorithm of flexibility and predictability. For example, wholesale retailer Costco employs more than 112,000 people, and 90 percent of them are hourly employees. Respect for workers' needs has been a key part of Costco's culture for the last twenty-seven years, and has yielded excellent results for the company. Better than 50 percent of its workers are full time, a by-product of Costco management doing its best to ensure workers have predictable schedules in order to be able to better coordinate their work with their other responsibilities. In addition, part-time workers are given a minimum of twenty-four hours of work a week and receive their schedules a minimum of one week in advance, once again to provide as much predictability as possible. The result? Costco's employee turnover is currently an admirable 10 percent and it is the most productive retailer in the country.[17]

Successfully offering flexibility (and predictability at the same time) to hourly workers requires careful thought and attention to the differences hourly workers face in challenges with their schedules in order to avoid well-meant policies that backfire with unintended consequences. In studying retailers that offer hourly workers a chance to declare which days and shifts they are available for work—an arrangement that at first glance appears to be a positive move toward offering hourly workers flexibility—Lambert found that workers who took advantage of the policy were simply being scheduled for fewer hours by their managers looking for easy coverage. These workers *do* get more flexibility, but take an often-untenable financial hit.[18] And while some salaried workers and professionals might desire a nontraditional schedule that would allow them flexibility, for workers most likely to work swing shifts or other nonstandard hours, including those in electronics manufacturing, food service, financial services, and retail sales, many would prefer a more standard arrangement.[19] It's a complicated issue to work through, made more complicated by the lack of people who spend their time on this sector of employees and their managers. Yet for hourly workers and the companies that employ them, win-win solutions are possible (see sidebar), and we hope that success stories like Costco inspire more attention.

A SIMPLE SOLUTION THAT MADE A DIFFERENCE

It is possible to create flexible schedules that accommodate both employers and hourly workers. One study looked to improve flexibility outcomes for workers of a Chicago retailer. From the outset, the study acknowledged that retail is a 24/7 business with high sales during evenings and weekends, when many workers are able to shop. Researchers finally settled on the advance notice of schedules as the best place to look for improvements, allowing for workers to plan appropriately and work out family and personal responsibilities and managers to better plan for appropriate staffing levels.[20] In the pilot study, the Chicago retailer posted schedules further in advance, improving and formalizing the communication system between workers and managers about preferred work hours and ongoing availability for extra shifts, a change that worked to everyone's benefit. The study results demonstrate the importance of taking the whole business—not just the worker's needs, not just the employer's needs—and an employee's full life—not just the work product—into account. It also demonstrates that employers need not spend money in order to save money and better workers' lives.

From Policy to Reality

The positive experiences enjoyed by the companies and workers described in this chapter are not accidents; they are the norm for those who offer flexible work arrangements. Just 18 percent of companies offering them perceive financial costs to outweigh benefits, while 65 to 76 percent of managers (depending on the question) report that policies like flexible work schedules have a positive or very positive impact on productivity, quality of work, and employee retention—with no change in the managers' workloads.[21]

Flexible work arrangements are also being used successfully as another way to attract, retain, and engage talent, according to Hewitt Associates, a global human resources services company.

In a survey of ninety U.S. employers, 66 percent said flexible programs increased employee engagement, 64 percent said they improved employee retention, and another 49 percent cited enhanced recruitment. And yet, according to Stanford professor Jeffrey Pfeffer, "in spite of the fact that much of what is required to build engaged and successful organizations is at once well known and not always costly to implement, many, maybe most, organizations have failed to take appropriate actions, thereby, in some sense, 'leaving money on the table.'"[22] Why do so many companies fail to give these policies a try, or ignore them once they're on the books? Why do most employers lack the structure or support to maximize the value that these programs offer?[23]

WORKERS CHOOSE LESS FLEX IN RECESSION

During a recession, the number of employees working flexibly at their own request usually stalls or declines. The number of tele-commuters dipped during the 2001 recession, then recovered, only to decline to 8.7 million in 2009 from 9.2 million in 2006 according to IDC, a Massachusetts research concern.[24] Contrary to what you might think, this trend isn't prompted by the employers but by the employees, who fear that asking for special work arrangements could hurt them in hard economic times.

The Boston College Center for Work & Family conducted an examination of businesses that had found success adopting flexible work arrangements and published the findings in "Overcoming the Implementation Gap: How 20 Leading Companies are Making Flexibility Work." The research revealed that it wasn't enough to promote or herald innovative flexible strategies or to print them in an HR manual. The programs and policies needed to be usable and effective for all in order to do any good. This discrepancy between the availability of these policies and their effective use is what the Center calls the "implementation gap."

There are a range of reasons why the implementation gap exists; it's unfortunate that too often people can't take advantage of existing options because of real or perceived bias. Even seemingly enlightened employers that offer work-life policies might not be entirely consistent in their application to all employees in all jobs. "Across a range of sectors—in law firms, media companies, and investment banks—we found that women (and men) perceive many work-life policies (telecommuting, job sharing, part-time or flexible jobs) as essentially 'off-limits' at their company," writes economist and author Sylvia Ann Hewlett, adding, "even if they are offered as corporate policy."[25]

In practice, the implementation gap is a familiar scenario. The experience of Carlos, a law firm associate, is proof of this type of bait-and-switch, whether the flexibility comes wrapped in a benefits package or results from a negotiated schedule. Though parental leave was touted as a benefit when he was hired, when Carlos tried to arrange for time off following the birth of his child, he was told in no uncertain terms that the policy was really just meant for women, and couldn't his (working) wife or his mother take care of his son? Carlos had chosen the firm in part because of benefits like paternity leave and a lower threshold for billable hours, which had spoken to him of the firm's commitment to its employees' whole lives. The response he faced, therefore, was disappointing on several levels and left a bitter taste that has never dissipated.

Similarly, Ben and Alicia thought they had it all: upwardly mobile lives, professional success, postgraduate education, and hard-charging jobs. Like so many people, they found their perspective changed with the arrival of children and learned how bias can affect men who want to work reduced schedules. Ben was already on the cutting edge when he chose to take the three-month parenting leave offered him, despite being on a partnership track at a prestigious law firm. Then he discovered how much he relished being a guiding force in his son's life, not a weekend parent. So Ben left the large firm for one that allowed some of its attorneys to work four-day weeks. Like Carlos, Ben soon found out the firm meant it, but only if you were a mother. Still Ben didn't give up, trying to arrange for yet another configuration that would help everyone get what they needed. When his third child was born, he suggested that instead of taking the traditional two weeks' paternity leave the firm offered, he would take the next ten Fridays off after the baby was born. After the work pattern was established—and it had been found to work well—Ben was able to continue the arrangement at 80 percent pay.

Yet Ben has had to fight for his custom fit every step of the way, finding flexibility less available to him because of the combination of his sex and his reason: caretaking. "This was the first time that, as a white male, I could recall experiencing being faced with unfair bias at work. I had this theory that the only obstacle to getting the schedule I wanted was in my head, but that clearly wasn't true." He adds that pressure "wasn't coming from the human resources department; it was coming from outdated gender stereotypes, held by my managers, about what men are supposed to be doing."[26]

What is often behind the failure to truly embrace employee-friendly custom-fit policies, or the failure to offer policies that create meaningful change, are managers and executives who equate asking for a reduced schedule—or for flexible scheduling or remote work options—with shirking responsibility. The two examples just highlighted were both men and both attorneys; we chose those stories intentionally to show the range of obstacles met by workers with much in common. It's not just men, of course; between one-quarter and one-third of women report coming up against roadblocks to using flexible work arrangements in the corporate culture of their organizations.[27] Extend just the issue of bias out to encompass all workers and every reason behind a custom fit, and the obstacles are endless, as you probably already know too well.

So if we know that the implementation gaps exist, and the ultimate goal is to work toward creating a custom fit for every worker, it can feel daunting to take on the challenge of bridging that gap. Yet we feel that the workers and managers of today are up for the challenge, and that doing so will require a combination of culture change (facing down those old stereotypes and practices) and practical tactics: using the best of what's working out there right now—practices, implementation strategies, ideas, and negotiated contracts. It means including everyone in the conversation, from hourly and union workers to managers to CEOs from the private, public, and nonprofit sectors.

The good news is that we don't have to reinvent the wheel. In putting together "Overcoming the Implementation Gap," the Boston College Center for Work & Family highlighted and relied upon the tips and best practices from those twenty companies finding success with flexibility to offer a primer on how best to overcome the gap. Here is a synopsis of those recommendations:

Address Management Resistance:

- At least one manager needs to champion the policy in the company and provide ongoing support as the initiative unfolds.
- Understand managers' fears and address them directly. Many are easily allayed through information or communication.
- Provide training for everyone involved, including offering real-life examples and success stories and covering the business case both thoroughly and convincingly.

- Use scenarios to explore the limitations and possibilities of flexible policies or management changes. Problem-solve proactively for any difficulties that might arise.

- Enable and encourage the use of outcome-based performance goals instead of depending on "face time"—time spent meeting or communicating in person—to determine employee success.

- Flexibility is the key to custom fit in more ways than one. It is useful and empowering to give managers some discretion in the use of flexible policies. *Note:* This does not mean penalizing a certain class of workers to benefit others, or pinning consideration on criteria like gender, as in Ben's and Carlos's examples.

- Don't make managers go it alone. Encourage collaborative efforts and empower employees to communicate needs and ideas and influence their managers and their management practices. Many a great idea had its genesis with the employee instead of the CEO or the union boss.

- Flexibility and change need to work for both workers and their employers. A win-win scenario is a must.

Address Employee Skepticism and Fear:

- Give great examples, including success stories where the workers involved look just like those who would be affected. People identify with stories and good outcomes, and that excites people and gets them to try something new.

- Maintain flexibility around flexibility. Yes, it's not just managers who fear that a one-size-fits-all policy will affect their ability to do their job in the best way possible. Allow for discretion for managers and employees to work out custom fits that are tailored to them.

- Make sure the policies and practices are "reason-free." This helps fight the issue of not having a good enough reason to have a custom fit, and avoids anyone having to decide whether the worker who wants to spend time with a church group or the worker who wants to coach Little League or the worker who wants to do a triathlon have worthy enough goals to deserve good integration between work and life.

- Have commitment and support from the top that shows. If employees believe that managers are behind custom-fit practices, they are more likely to embrace the idea themselves.

Address Resistance to Change:

- Encourage and support new ways of thinking and behaving. Reordering the priorities of a workplace takes more than issuing a memo. Look to the root of the organization culture and work to effect change there.

- Aim large, but set realistic expectations. Realize that, depending on the change being implemented and the scale, it can be very difficult to overcome entrenched philosophies, ideas, practices, and stereotypes. Expect change to take months or even years.

- Help others deconstruct the reasoning behind the program. Help them see that the core problem behind the implementation gap isn't just a lack of trust, it's the traditional work model on which our economy has been based.[28]

In addition to the excellent points outlined in the study, there are more concrete recommendations from those who have found success blazing the custom-fit workplace path. It all begins with commitment to change, needed by both someone on the management team—it doesn't have to be the CEO at first—and the employees involved. Once a company is committed to action, it should research the needs of the business—is it facing high turnover? Absenteeism? Rising overhead costs?—and the needs of the employees—are they crushed by useless meetings? Trapped in a standard schedule? Unable to balance work and family?— before crafting policy. Third, the flexible policies must be flexible themselves, and allow room for exceptions, changes, and for managers to use their professional abilities to meet situational needs. Finally, and perhaps most important, all concerned need to recognize a culture shift is afoot; both business and employees need to believe that flexibility and work-life integration are advantages for the workplace of the future and are attainable goals.[29]

Success Stories

Change can be sparked by an individual business owner who wants to make life better for the workforce; by a single employee who is determined to have balance; or by an organization that is savvy enough to ask its employees how work could improve. Though we offer scores more of these success stories throughout the book, here are three that we find most compelling to get you in the mood.

Jim Johnson, introduced at the beginning of this chapter, implemented many of the custom-fit arrangements covered in this book, starting with work-from-home, a flexible workweek, and job sharing. At Johnson Moving & Storage, the workers' flexible hours are set by the associates themselves, not by the company. Workers are paid the same hourly rate whether they work full time or part time. Perhaps most important, no stigma is attached to employees who take advantage of any of the policies.[30] Jim also implemented performance reviews that take into account whether or not the job is getting done, not who has spent the most time at work. Jim offers a striking example not just of an employer who has implemented and stood behind these policies, but an employer who has exhibited respect for his workers and afforded the employer-employee relationship the dignity it deserves.

REQUESTING FLEX: SOME TIPS

According to Jim Johnson, owner of Johnson Moving & Storage, if you are an employee asking for flexible options, these are the tips to keep in mind:

- Plan how you will be able to get your job done
- Put it in writing
- Keep the request professional, not personal—that is, focus on the benefits that accrue to the business
- Suggest a trial period
- Set an end date for evaluation[31]

Like any business proposition, focus on how both you and your employer benefit from the work arrangement you propose.

Though top-level support is necessary for success, change sometimes originates with the employees themselves. In many cases, one employee begins the process by asking for a creative solution to a work-life conflict. Positive results then create the momentum (and precedent) for more systemic change throughout the organization. For example, job sharing was instituted at KPMG LLP, the U.S. arm of the international auditing firm with nearly 100,000 employees, because two individuals asked to reduce hours and share a position. After finding success through a few pilot arrangements, the company launched a formalized program that was part of its initiative to promote flexibility, wellness, and diversity.[32]

Our last story highlights a company that took it upon itself to ask employees about their job satisfaction, and then *listened*— and did something about it. MITRE is a nonprofit with expertise in systems engineering, information technology, and operational concepts whose research and development centers work with the Department of Defense, the Federal Aviation Administration, and the Internal Revenue Service. MITRE's nearly six thousand employees took a survey that asked about their work-life satisfaction. In the survey results, two of the company's practices stood out as particular negatives: the mandate for a fixed five-day workweek and the requirement to take full-day absences for missing an hour or two of work, even if the time was made up.

MITRE paid attention. The company implemented and offered a menu of many of the flexible work arrangements outlined in this chapter for employees to choose from, with about 90 percent participation in the program. By making flexibility *flexible*, MITRE reduced its attrition rate to 3 percent—and productivity remained steady. Now, workers rank flexibility as their top reason for choosing to work there. One of MITRE's satisfied workers is Tom Ervin, a principal engineer in the Cyber Analysis and Investigations department. Not only was Tom able to retain his job through two geographical moves, he was able to take on primary care of his son while his wife was on active duty in the military, and even volunteered in his son's school (running a chess program)—all while earning more technical awards than before the policies were in place. Through thoughtful analysis and listening to the needs of its workforce, MITRE has literally changed lives while attracting and retaining the top talent it needs.

Johnson Moving & Storage, KPMG, and MITRE serve as inspirations for us all to get into gear, as the stories of individual workers like April, Cindy, and Joan Turano show us that change is not only possible, it's positive. And these examples of standard flexible practices represent only the beginning—there are far more cutting-edge, creative approaches to customizing work arrangements. And even these basic practices can be pushed to new heights.

Imagine the compressed-workweek scenario, and then imagine it stretched further for, say, a worker who wants summers free to travel with a schoolteacher spouse. Or the part-time worker who ramps back up to full-time during busy seasons or during periods when more income is needed. There are a vast number of ways of working that people and organizations have yet to explore to make the custom-fit workplace a reality. It's time for that good old American ingenuity to kick into high gear and make it possible.

4

VIRTUALLY PERFECT

The Promises of Remote Work

Imagine a future in which a whole generation of Americans "go to work" by padding in stocking-feet to well-equipped rooms in their homes, booting up their computers, and joining their coworkers online. They might videoconference with a client in the morning, submit a final draft of a report on a secured server in the afternoon, and, before logging off for the day, send a series of instant messages to a colleague who's falling behind on a deadline. These workers groan at stories of their elders' hour-long bumper-to-bumper commutes, the equivalent of "*I walked three miles in the snow just to get to school*" of our own grandparents. You've just imagined the virtual work generation, a generation descending upon us at lightning speed.

In fact, virtual workers already exist, and in growing numbers. According to a Dieringer Research Group study, 17.2 million Americans worked remotely at least one day per month in 2008, an increase of 39 percent from 2006 and *74 percent* since 2005.[1] Virtual workers are defined as people who work from home, from the road, from anywhere that isn't a traditional centralized office. The common denominator for all virtual workers is that they communicate and perform their duties almost entirely through electronic technology.[2]

A simple phone line and Internet connectivity now allow employees to connect, collaborate, and conduct business from remote settings (most commonly a home work space, though we recommend a beach blanket if you can swing it). Technology that supports virtual work ranges from the most basic—your trusty phone and modem—to more complex systems with fire-walls and other safeguards to protect company or client data, intranets, sophisticated videoconferencing, and more.

Going virtual makes sense for many workers, not just the hip writer-types you see plugging in at coffee shops around the country: Gen Ys just starting out, older workers phasing into retirement, people who need flexibility because they have restricted physical abilities, live in remote locations, or live in two-job households where being close to both jobs is impossible—all have embraced this new way to work. And while highly paid professionals relish the ability to e-mail from their smart phones and do videoconferencing from a mountain-top retreat, it's also being used effectively by workers in lower-wage jobs. For example, call centers, which tend to be crowded and stressful when located in large, cubicle-packed office buildings, can become peaceful, environmentally low-impact, and even family-friendly when located in workers' homes. For these workers, too, the ability to manage the rest of one's life, work a more custom schedule, and avoid the expense and time of commuting holds high value. In fact, according to a survey on worker productivity, nearly 60 percent of employees believe that telecommuting at least part time is the ideal work situation.[3]

Virtual work makes sense for employers, too, whether it's a large company like IBM or a few individuals launching a start-up. As noted in Chapter Three, scores of organizations—from government offices to large companies—have already incorporated remote work into their emergency preparedness plans, recognizing its ability to inoculate businesses against productivity losses resulting from pandemics, floods, snowstorms, and power outages.

And it can create a more robust business overall, as virtual work has been shown to cut workplace costs and produce happier, more productive workers. Testifying in front of Congress on the benefits of virtual work, Lexis Nexis Director of Field Operations-East Debra McKenzie reported increases in employee productivity of 20 to 25 percent, particularly in technological areas.[4] Those who work virtually for American Express produce 43 percent more business than their office counterparts.[5] Making large-scale business improvements like reorganizing or moving a headquarters can be very expensive. In comparison, the improvement of adjusting to a virtual work world can use easily available technology with no real-estate costs. IBM, for example, saves $700 million in real estate costs by allowing 25 percent of its employees worldwide to work from home.[6]

But you don't have to run a multimillion-dollar business to see the virtue in virtual; virtual work also appeals to budding entrepreneurs. The business consultant who always wanted to start a firm can feel empowered to do so, setting work hours and hiring others to help without the high overhead of office space.

Virtual work makes sense, which is why the number of business sectors embracing it is rapidly expanding. Though it doesn't work for all types of organizations, teams, and workers, it can be used far more widely than it is being used now, offering greater flexibility to more people. More than that, technological advancements and business policies that promote and enable virtual work have the capability to reshape the business landscape as we know it, promoting greater work-life fit, advancing a healthier environmental agenda, cutting costs, and improving business outcomes and practices. Virtual work opens up all kinds of possibilities for workers who need flexibility and businesses that need to compete in this ever-changing global economy—an economy in which human talent and technology will reign.

Employers that ignore the possibilities currently offered by technology risk more than just losing out on an affordable, creative way to offer flexibility and increase profits. They risk becoming obsolete in the workplace of the future.

Remember those who ignored VHS, sure Betamax would survive? We didn't think so.

The Virtual Work Continuum

We find it helpful to think of the full range of virtual work arrangements as falling on a continuum. At one end we have what we call "the virtual individual"—an arrangement wherein a person works remotely, usually on an ad hoc basis, even for a company that has an established headquarters, and even if other colleagues do not use a similar setup. This might be a city employee who works from home occasionally when the kids are off on a school holiday, or someone who arranges to work remotely when a spouse is transferred across the country. This is where we begin our study of virtual work.

Next, there are entire divisions or departments within a company that work remotely, a situation we've dubbed "the virtual team." In a virtual team arrangement, 90 percent of the company may operate from, say, Atlanta, while the sales staff is spread around the country or work with a global team with members in fifteen countries. A large corporation might center its manufacturing in one area but allow call center employees to work from their homes. Unlike the virtual individual, the virtual team usually finds its genesis with the company, not with the worker, and employees are able to take advantage of business and communication systems specially designed to promote their remote work.

And finally, on the far side of the continuum we find "the virtual organization," a more unusual setup in today's business world but one with many attributes worth a second look. This is an organization designed with no physical headquarters, in which every individual who works there and every new hire is a virtual worker. The way people in virtual organizations do it, and the benefits and challenges they encounter, may hint at new kinds of workplaces in the future.

By demonstrating that virtual work is not an all-or-nothing proposition, our hope is that you see yourself or your employees in at least one of the examples of success presented in this chapter, or that they prompt you to think creatively about ways that virtual work might operate in your own life or workplace.

The Virtual Individual

Many companies don't feel a pressing need or desire to adopt virtual work practices. That is, until life intervenes and threatens to steal away a valuable employee, an employee the company invested in for years with the expectation of a career-long relationship. When a worker's life intervenes, it may come in the form of a spouse being transferred out of the area, or an ailing parent needing care, or medical difficulties demanding attention—anything that would keep that worker from going to the office on a regular basis, and that without accommodation might prompt a resignation.

Enter the virtual individual, an employee permitted to work virtually while the rest of the company occupies a street address and probably houses a water cooler or two. Would-be virtual individuals may not have company policy to rely on, but rather need to negotiate with their manager or employer and iron out the specifics on a case-by-case basis. As with all custom-fit options, negotiation and compromise are key elements. The employer might now expect daily phone calls, whereas when working together in the office it didn't always seem necessary to check in on such a frequent basis. The employee might ask the employer to pay for wireless service or other expenses that might have previously been covered out-of-pocket.

There are challenges to the virtual individual arrangement, most prompted by the probability that the company's communication and management systems have not anticipated the need. It may take the manager extra time or require extra organizational forethought to make sure the virtual individual is appropriately looped in on important information, such as setting up a conference call or videoconferencing instead of rounding up people on the fly to work out an issue. And the employee may have to spend more time on tasks that used to be covered by walking down the hall to ask another department for help, such as tech trouble-shooting. It may prove necessary to work harder to combat a tendency toward "out of sight, out of mind" and stay in touch with the work group and its manager. Virtual individuals can also face changes in the way they need to communicate; lacking face-to-face contact they may need to restate issues and goals and make sure communication is clear. They may also fight feelings of isolation.

It's not always seamless, but the payoffs for both parties make the arrangement worthwhile. Many virtual workers report higher productivity in part because of an absence of distractions, and the use of sick leave by remote employees tends to decline.[7] In fact, virtual workers appear measurably healthier, more connected to their communities, and less stressed. They have more freedom to pursue important goals or flexibility to attend to emergency family responsibilities. The choice is so coveted by some that a survey of Canadian workers by EKOS Research Associates showed 43 percent would quit their current employer for a job that allowed virtual work arrangements, and 35 percent of survey respondents would trade some salary for the option.[8] Conversely, when employers adapt to their employees' changing life circumstances, that respect for the employee in turn fosters loyalty, improving the odds for retention.

Davis is a great example of how that loyalty plays out in the end. He is now a thirty-year-old engineer working on site for a large software company, but at twenty-six he had already worked for the company for five years, managing a small group of software developers. Davis was enjoying a rewarding and promising career when he and his wife jointly decided to spend time abroad before fully "settling down into adulthood." Davis's wife is a teacher, a profession that affords her a host of good foreign exchange opportunities, and she was eventually offered the opportunity to teach in Eastern Europe for a year. Before she went through the application process, Davis notified his managers of his intent and asked if it would be possible for him to work remotely for the year. He knew the answer might be no; his employer does not routinely offer virtual work positions, and it requires development managers to work on site. Though he enjoyed his career, Davis was prepared to resign so as to pursue the overseas experience important to him and his wife at a time in their lives when living abroad seemed possible.

Davis was somewhat surprised to find both of his managers supportive of the idea of him working abroad, though neither was entirely sure how the logistics would work. Davis was used to working on site, with his peers and reports in easy reach, and both his work environment and the management models of the company supported that system. The company had a wide variety of tools for business communication with remote teams in India, for example, but its management structure didn't support or encourage virtual meetings or remote problem-solving with individuals outside of e-mail. Face-to-face meetings with managers happened at least on a weekly basis, as did team meetings with four or five colleagues working on the same project. Impromptu work problems were solved by gathering engineers in a room to talk issues through and then mapping out computer code on white boards. While manager-report "one on ones" could be done by phone, it was hard to see how other systems could be replicated if Davis worked off site. Indeed, replicating the value of off-the-cuff collaboration and the ease of in-person communication is a drawback to virtual work, especially for virtual members of an otherwise on-site team. By some estimates as much as 30 percent of a senior manager's time is spent in hallway or parking lot conversations, strengthening relationships and leading to collaboration and innovation.[9]

Still, just because the company's infrastructure wasn't set up to support virtual work didn't mean that Davis's request was out of reach. His position was shifted to more readily accommodate the constraints within the company structure. His job description was changed so that he no longer managed other engineers—a role that really did require face time—and he was given largely independent tasks that could easily be executed without physical presence. Though the task was challenging at times, his managers' willingness to develop a virtual work situation for him enabled Davis to stay with the company (and his wife!), contribute to the team, and pursue an important life goal. His managers were pleased with the arrangement, as they were able to retain Davis and his skills for little cost and effort. Davis returned, and now works on site for the same employer, managing a group of seven. His current manager describes him as "a stellar employee with an excellent career trajectory ahead of him," adding that he's glad they were able to make it work so that Davis stayed with the company. "It would not be in our best interest if a competitor got the benefit of his talents instead of us."

Davis is an example of a person who wanted to temporarily work remotely to fit together his on-the-job and personal priorities. Virtual work made it possible for him to fulfill his aspiration to live abroad while young and his need to stay close to his wife to support her hope of teaching in a foreign exchange program for a year. For many organizations, virtual arrangements find their genesis in similar situations, granting individual workers permission to work remotely on a case-by-case basis, either full time, a few days a week, or on an as-needed basis. It may then become a standard custom-fit policy option as both management and workers become familiar with the advantages and learn how to accommodate the differences successfully.

FROM TELECOMMUTING TO TELEPRESENCE

Sure, there's face time and teleconferencing. But how do you combine the best of both worlds—the instant communication of on-site work with all the benefits of virtual? You inhabit the body of a robot, of course.

Dallas Goercker lives in Indiana and works in California's Silicon Valley at a company called Willow Garage that, yes, happens to develop hardware and software for personal robotic applications. Dallas's coworkers know him well—they talk to him daily, they interact with him in the hallway, they stop him to tell him he's needed in a meeting in the conference room—only they know him as Texas, the robot. Texas navigates and communicates through a webcam, a monitor that pivots to change the view, a laser scanner, and an additional camera to keep an eye on the road. In an ABC news report, Dallas's boss said that initially the idea seemed unnecessary, but that in the end "it turns out it makes a huge difference in how we know Dallas." Dallas agrees, adding that his coworkers not only have gotten to know him better, and vice versa, but that "they like to dress me up, they like to put stickers on me, all around."[10]

Thus far, so-called "telepresence robots" are used almost exclusively in medical care, allowing remote doctors to "round" on patients. They're also starting to be used in education. Research centers from the United States to Japan focus on robots like Texas that can stand in as a physical presence for a remote worker, and are introducing helper bots that can aid the elderly in their homes and even go shopping for them.

What would you name *your* robot?

Like Davis, George initially asked for a temporary virtual work arrangement. A programmer at a well-known computer company when his elderly father fell ill, he requested and was granted the flexibility to work from home. This allowed him to provide help not only to his father but also to his mother, who was his father's caregiver. The temporary arrangement evolved into a permanent one. Upon his father's death, George asked to continue the arrangement in order to stay available to his elderly mother. George's situation speaks to one attraction remote working holds for the growing cohort of workers—one third of the current workforce—caring for an older family member. While no one expects (or wants) workers to be performing job duties and caregiving at the same time—be that with parents or children—the increased availability and flexibility is incredibly important for those in this situation.

Janine, on the other hand, began her position as a district sales manager for a mobile phone manufacturing company as a remote worker. Though the company has its headquarters in southern California, when she was hired she lived in Chicago and worked virtually from her home office. Several times a year she would travel to California for strategic meetings with top management, but the rest of the time she connected to the company's intranet—or internal company files—first via phone lines and later using the Internet. Her direct reports were salespeople in her district who communicated with her via phone and e-mail. Only occasionally did they need face-to-face meetings.

It is perhaps not surprising that computer and phone manufacturers would be early adopters of virtual work arrangements for employees. Because they develop and understand communication technology, they may feel comfortable or adept at being at the cutting edge of workplace practices that take advantage of it, at least for individual workers who need work-life solutions and request them. Yet there's not always a corollary relationship, as Davis's case proves. His workplace was ultimately very supportive, but his managers didn't have a virtual work support system in place when Davis made his request.

Even mega-technology companies can do more to support virtual work situations through management practices that deemphasize face time and by being thoughtful with their technological resources. And remember Erin, the hospital administrator, from Chapter One? Though she did not work in the communication technology field, a virtual arrangement was easily accessible to her. And she's not alone. In a 2008 survey, 70 percent of workers who do not currently work remotely said that 20 percent or more of their job duties could be performed successfully at home.[11]

The Virtual Team

When virtual arrangements apply not just to a single worker but to an entire team, operation, or division of a traditional company, we call that "the virtual team." Virtual team work can require more infrastructure than your standard team arrangement, both in technology and planned communication strategies. It is the latter point that is perhaps the most challenging to overcome. In the early 1980s, Hewlett-Packard popularized what came to be known as MBWA (management by walking around), allowing bosses to have more casual encounters with employees, eliciting better responses from shrinking violets who might not speak up in large groups and establishing a less formal relationship that encouraged communication.[12] Virtual teams must be managed more deliberately and communication organized in a way that can take more time and need to be more frequent. Global teams and time zone differences complicate the picture even more. While 24/7 availability for tech support is great on the one hand, scheduling a meeting between workers on teams in London, Tel Aviv, San Francisco, and Mumbai poses more of a challenge. How do you allow virtual workers in four time zones, each several hours apart from all the others, to feel inspired and part of the company when the president is speaking on site to the rest of the employees?

Nonetheless, successful companies have addressed the downside of not sharing the same physical space—from virtual "desks" with kids' photos and personal information to using technology to interact in real time with employees—and benefited from the upside. In the end, studies show that when a company successfully establishes virtual teams, the rewards come in the form of happier, more productive employees, lowered costs, and access to a wide, talented workforce.

In one of the most oft-cited precedents of companies making a move to virtual teams, U.S. airline JetBlue created an entirely virtual customer-service call center, using fifteen hundred home-based employees to handle approximately thirty-five thousand calls each day. This workforce is not based in a developing country nor even near the company headquarters in New York; it is in Utah. Basing the virtual workers there allows JetBlue to tap into an often-overlooked talent pool; 60 percent of the call center's staff members are women with children under eighteen years of age, women who need work they can do from home on either a full-time or part-time basis. The remaining 40 percent of JetBlue's virtual workforce is made up of retirees and students. As an additional benefit, the students JetBlue is able to hire because of this work arrangement are fluent in Spanish and able to communicate with Spanish-speaking callers. Tapping into a larger talent pool enables this company to better serve the needs of all its clients.

Similar to JetBlue, the company 1-800 Contacts also moved half of its 320-person call center operations team to a work-from-home virtual arrangement in Utah, a move that allowed for flexibility for the customer service representatives and that meant increased profits and productivity for the company. When J.D. Power and Associates certified the call center, surveys showed that its overall satisfaction index score was the highest index score achieved in the call center certification program, with the strength of the company's customer service representatives, general call center operations, and problem resolution receiving special mention.

CareGroup CIO John Halamka also credits JetBlue's pioneering efforts in virtual teams with inspiring his company's pilot virtual work program for the medical record coders at Beth Israel Deaconess Medical Center in Boston. Like the two companies already discussed, the medical center had strong business incentives for designing the pilot program, not only for the medical record coders who would enjoy the freedom of working remotely but also for the call center employees and desktop engineering team. The first incentive had to do with the available talent pool. Medical coders were in short supply in Boston; taking the work virtual enabled the group to cast a wider net for experienced coders across the country. The engineering team was able to enjoy the peace and quiet of a remote location, boosting its ability to focus and concentrate. In tackling the pilot projects, Halamka had reservations, but was ultimately won over. Halamka's article detailing his experience with taking teams virtual, "How I Learned to Stop Worrying and Love Telecommuting," gives a preview of his conclusions after surveying and experimenting with virtually every technology system available during the 2008 project.[13] In the end, Halamka came to believe remote work was not only possible—both for him personally and for various teams—but in fact necessary. (See sidebar for a synopsis of technological systems and products that help aid virtual work.)

TECHNOLOGICAL TOOLS TO EMPOWER VIRTUAL WORK

The day-to-day needs of many virtual workers are met with readily available (and often free!) software, programs, and equipment. For others, and for some businesses investing in virtual team structures, more creative and specially designed systems and technology are necessary. CareGroup CIO John Halamka found providing the infrastructure support necessary for at-home work was just the beginning for him. Because of the inherently sensitive nature of dealing with personal medical histories, privacy and security questions loomed large. In the end, Halamka was able to implement a system that allowed for continuous, reliable data sharing with a high level of security. Here is a sample of what works:

- Company-provided computers and Internet connections
- Smart phones, such as BlackBerrys and iPhones, for on-the-go e-mail and phone contact
- IM (instant messaging) platforms to allow for virtual chat
- Videoconferencing

Continued

- Blogging
- Documentation *wikis*, Web sites that allow multiple users to easily post information
- Secure file transfer protocol that allows for safe and functional file access, transfer, and management between remote workers and a company server
- Remote presentation tools

Depending on the type of work and the size of the business, a host of technological advances can work similarly for companies interested in working virtually more effectively.

The Virtual Organization

In the last ten years, some entirely virtual organizations have emerged, including software services providers Chorus and We Also Walk Dogs, as well as grassroots organizers MoveOn and (our very own) MomsRising. This means they have no physical headquarters or regional offices, and employees are distributed throughout the city or the country, or the world, working wherever they please. The work they are assigned must get done, but where it's done is irrelevant.

MoveOn, the Internet-based nonprofit advocacy organization with five million members and counting, is a pioneer as an entirely virtual organization. Its organizers have even created a policy known as "the MoveOn Way," a model where virtual work is not just a benefit but intrinsic to the organization, part of its basic nature. The MoveOn model may seem extreme to some: MoveOn rejects mixing virtual and nonvirtual work and insists its core team of twenty works remotely, to the point where organizational policy precludes workers from sharing office space. (A caveat: MoveOn has granted one exception to this rule to date for very family-friendly reasons, allowing co-founders Joan Blades and Wes Boyd to live together as a married couple and work from the same house.) Why should a few MoveOn members who happen to all live in, say, New York, be denied the opportunity to share an office space? The philosophy behind the rule stems in part from the expectation that if a group of staff are working in the same office, that group would inevitably and unintentionally fail to include the online group in significant conversations—conversations that the group typically must engage in online. This would then replicate the difficulties Davis's employer saw in having some staff off site and thereby out of one or more information or decision loops.

An additional benefit of the virtual organization is one many see as a drawback: people communicate exclusively through technology. This remote communication requires clear development and articulation of goals, reliable follow-up, and thoughtful information-sharing practices—something that would be beneficial to most any organization, but the nature of virtual work makes it critical.

MoveOn takes pride in being nimble. Like a news organization, it must be quick to respond to events of the day, which requires timely and detailed team communication. To manage a very active (and some might say overwhelming) internal e-mail stream (which includes extensive sharing of ideas, news, brainstorming, status updates, and even personal stories in addition to the pressing collaborative work of the day), it has devised a coded system to make it easy for people to prioritize what they will read and respond to. Both team members and long-term contractors are able to engage in rich online dialogue and collaboration while still efficiently determining what they should be focusing on.

MoveOn has found this work style is also good for working with the many partner organizations, contractors, and engaged volunteers the organization needs in order to do its work on a national scale. As mentioned in Chapter Three, performance-based management styles aid in the implementation of flexible practices like virtual work; in this case, where the flexible work policy guides the organization, leadership believes that the necessary discipline coupled with the transparent and flat management structure is in fact more efficient than traditional management practices.

MoveOn has noted another related benefit to the all-virtual model: its people are invested in further mastering technology and systems to enhance virtual work organization-wide (instead of trying to patch together technologies for a handful of remote workers). Staying on the cutting edge of technology as well as innovating formats for remote brainstorming, collaborative decision making, and retreats has not only facilitated day-to-day operations, it has also made the organization a leader in the world of grassroots organizing.

Last but not least, a virtual organization means office politics and even unintentional human dominance behaviors are largely short-circuited. This is an environment where people are each known for what they contribute to the team. There is no problem with messy people or noisy people, and not much motivation to talk behind anyone's back. Moreover, how tall you are, how well you dress, and even how much seniority you have are less apparent in the virtual environment, where ideas and contributing to the team effort are the primary focus.

While you may not see your own job or position reflected in the MoveOn example, you can extract a universal lesson from its way of doing business. The organization as a whole embraces the benefits of virtual work. This is a philosophy shared by organizations that find success with virtual models; instead of seeing only logistical hurdles, they see possibility. While most organizations will never go so far as to prohibit employees from working in the same office, the core belief that remote work is valuable and effective is key to the team's success.

A virtual organization doesn't have to be the size of MoveOn; it can be an army of one—at least, to begin with. Kirsten was a thirty-nine-year-old single woman and a founding partner in a six-person public relations firm specializing in the food industry when things began to sour with the partnership. She planned to make a clean break from the firm and take a couple of months off. Three weeks into that break, Kirsten's phone started ringing. Potential clients who had heard of her work through the grapevine or who knew her through the restaurant industry wanted her help. She took it as a sign and started taking on clients, working from home. "In the beginning, it was just me, working part-time for one or two clients, no logo, on my cell phone and laptop," she reports, adding, "I had generic business cards made from a vendor on the Internet. I still had some meetings and did a lot of networking and soon I had a full client base."

Kirsten discovered that her new way of working was better than her old. She had more control over her schedule, more quiet time, enough space for writing press releases and materials, and breaks from the endless phone calls and meetings common in public relations work. She used the Internet to connect more deeply to the increasingly vibrant virtual world surrounding the restaurant industry—which helped her work better on behalf of her clients. "Right now restaurant buzz is about blogs, about online magazines and reviews, Twitter, and Google alerts. In a way, we're all trending virtual—except for the food, of course!"

When Kirsten's workload becomes too heavy, she hires help as needed. Working virtually is not only an option for her recruits—it's a requirement. In this way, small businesses throughout the country can grow and flourish and easily expand or contract their workforce quickly in response to the needs of clients or projects. Chapter Six explores this phenomenon in more depth, looking at various entrepreneurs and contractors who were able to leave rigid workplaces and create their own businesses or contract for other companies because of the inherent flexibility of virtual work.

The Benefits of Virtual Work

From Davis to Kirsten, from JetBlue to MoveOn, virtual work arrangements can take many forms. But what they all have in common is that they offer significant custom-fit benefits to employers and employees alike. Here are some of the ways both benefit from the opportunity to work virtually.

How Employers Benefit

For employers, the most prominent benefit of virtual work is the impact it has on the bottom line. AT&T, for example, drastically reduced its real estate costs when it allowed thirty thousand of its workers to telecommute regularly.

AT&T's comprehensive program, Alternative Officing, has been in development for several years. This project is particularly interesting because it includes a rigorous cost-benefit analysis of the company's North Central New Jersey site, in the form of a five-year study of six hundred telecommuters. The study found that the most substantial savings realized by Alternative Officing were in reduced real estate costs. By allowing employees to telecommute, AT&T was able to close an entire office complex, equaling annual real estate savings of more than $6 million.

In addition to hard cost savings, AT&T saw substantial productivity gains. Based on employee interviews, the company estimates a conservative gain of two and a half hours per employee per week in time worked. It attributed an annual gain of more than $5 million to increased productivity. Also, employees state almost without exception that they were able to be more productive during the hours they worked, due primarily to fewer interruptions, an annual efficiency boost that equates to more than $3 million saved.

There were, of course, costs associated with setting up employees to work at home. Office alterations averaged $3,000 per employee and computer and phone installations averaged $4,000 per employee. These costs were depreciated over five years, and $1,250 per employee per year was added for phone, fax, copy, and postage bills. AT&T determined these annual costs were somewhat more than $3 million.

Putting the exact numbers together, here's what Alternative Officing has meant for AT&T:

AT&T Cost Savings and Productivity Gains

Real Estate Savings	$6,333,124
Productivity Gains (Hours)	$5,112,841
Productivity Gains (Efficiency)	$3,127,617
Total	$14,573,582
Less Costs	(3,205,507)
Net Annual Gain	$11,368,075[14]

With gains of more than $11 million per year, AT&T is a shining example of the financial reasons why virtual work *works*.

Reduced operating costs and increased productivity and efficiency are clear-cut ways virtual work can help employers. Less obvious but equally significant are the ways in which the management shifts required by a virtual workforce can lead a company in the direction of increased profitability. Not only did 1-800 Contacts reduce operating costs by moving people off-site, the new style of management required by off-site workers helped save even more. The company employed a "business intelligence" technology program that helped it track results of call-center employees and provide real-time feedback to workers—the virtual version of walking the aisles and listening in on calls. Yet this same technology also pointed to different strategies to take with customers, the implementation of which boosted sales by $40,000 a month through improved closing ratios.[15]

AT&T and 1-800 Contacts both provide easily quantifiable ways virtual work saves dollars. Less quantifiable are the opportunities virtual work affords for a company to recruit and hire from a wider talent pool. Talented candidates who would not have been available because they needed flexible work, lived far from the hiring facility, or had some other limitation can now be hired. Examples include CareGroup, which was able to cast a wide net for medical record coders in short supply near the company's Boston headquarters. Additionally, a disability advocacy group reported that 10 percent of organizations hired new employees with disabilities to virtual jobs.[16] Both JetBlue and 1-800 Contacts take advantage of the availability of at-home parents in Utah to fill their jobs, tapping into a loyal and dedicated workforce.

VIRTUAL WORK CREATES A WIN-WIN FOR DISABLED WORKERS

Virtual jobs can prove a win-win for workers with disabilities or chronic and changing medical or physical conditions, including cancer, arthritis, stroke, heart or respiratory disease, chronic back injury, chronic pain, and mental health conditions. For many employees who face the sudden onset of illness, job retention can be difficult, as can spending long hours in an office and commuting. A study of 432 virtual-work-friendly employers conducted by the Midwest Institute for Telecommuting Education and the Humphrey Institute of Public Affairs showed that 25 percent of employers that currently practice virtual work offered the option to employees with disabilities; 71 percent of virtual workers with disabilities were employed full time.

Most offers of a remote work option were subject to the job duties being suitable and a supervisor's approval.[17]

Other benefits to organizations are a reduction of groupthink and office politics. This improves creativity and innovation, qualities needed increasingly in a world of global competition and rapid change.

Finally, workers value these jobs: They return to the employer accolades of "Best Places to Work" as well as loyalty and stability, which lower turnover costs. Workers show their appreciation with hard work and dedication, which enhances productivity. In addition, some students who are hired into flexible, part-time positions thank the company by accepting full-time positions upon graduation, with less training and start-up time required.

How Workers Benefit

So why do workers value these virtual positions so highly? What is it about virtual work that causes workers to reward their employers with loyalty and productivity? Nearly everyone we interviewed for this book listed flexibility to be with family at important moments as motivating factors for wanting virtual work; to this end, the importance of eliminating commute time cannot be overstated. Cutting commute time can give one, two, or even more hours a day back to family. Virtual work also benefits family members who want to take care of a sick parent who may live across the country, as George did.

In addition, having some control over aspects of work that don't affect productivity or end products—such as where you work—can lead to higher worker satisfaction. In a review of forty-six studies on remote work featuring a total of 12,883 employees, the increased autonomy of virtual work—from deciding how work gets done to choosing which podcast to listen to while working—resulted in more satisfied, productive workers who were less likely to quit their jobs.[18] If you want to wear your cozy slippers all day, you can. If you want to drink your home-brewed coffee instead of the office sludge, you can. If you want to use your usual lunch break to walk around the block or attend a school function, you can. In this way, virtual work combats burnout and stress. Though many forms of virtual work still require interaction with other people, it can be a godsend for people who work in noisy, bustling offices to have a little quiet time. Virtual work also creates a gentle way for people who have been out of the workforce to ramp back up into a career.

Stay Connected in Person Too

Even with all the benefits of virtual work for businesses and individuals, some people who work alone want more human contact during the day. They may crave interaction with like-minded people, spontaneous discussion, and the opportunity to use colleagues as a sounding board in an informal way. Many of the people we interviewed expressed the feeling that some face time could help ameliorate one of the most common pitfalls and concerns of virtual work: feeling disconnected and distant from the organization.

Christina has worked virtually for eight of the last ten years in the publishing industry, including in her current position with a small editorial and writing firm. Savvy with the ins and outs of virtual work, Christina joined the firm in part because she had worked virtually with her colleagues at a larger publishing house years before. Consequently, she says, she doesn't feel any sense of disconnect or distance from the company's collective operations, even though the other partners all work together in the main Seattle office. She credits their solid prior relationship with making it so easy to work remotely from her Portland home. On the other hand, she remembers being "totally disoriented" when she started a new job as the only virtual worker in a company that produced travel guides, with no one to talk to and no real way of getting a feel for the company. "It took me weeks to get in the groove and learn to trust my own instincts because I was working with so little feedback. Virtual work can be very difficult if you haven't already worked together with your colleagues at one point or another. You never have the chance to do the kind of bonding that I think is ultimately necessary if you're going to work somewhere long-term."

For some, there is simply no substitute for in-person interaction, and regular face time is necessary to make a (mostly) virtual position work. Ingrid, a teacher, has taught both live and online classes. Ingrid says, "There's something about the energy of the classroom that is spontaneous. You can get information from both, but the dynamics of a live classroom are inimitable and better, I think, than the best online chat." Ultimately, Ingrid says, her virtual/face-to-face hybrid allows her the best of both worlds, though if pressed to choose, virtual teaching would win out. "I'm so lucky to have the flexibility to do both," she adds. Ingrid has brought this synthesis to her work with her students, designing a curriculum for a virtual class that also meets in person to hear guest speakers and get in some face time.

As we've seen, business and technology systems that support virtual workers can reduce isolation and distance, as can active and thoughtful management. Even so, most organizations also support virtual systems with occasional face time to help workers connect. A study in the *Journal of Applied Psychology* supports this model, finding that occasional in-person meetings or get-togethers reduce feelings of isolation and encourage camaraderie.[19] JetBlue's virtual call center team is still asked to go into the main reservation center monthly for continuing education, staff meetings, and team-building exercises, and the company hosts an annual "family day" to boost morale. Ernst & Young's Americas Inclusiveness team, a virtual group with members in a number of locations, also meets in person once a year. Though an avowed advocate of the virtual-only model, MoveOn has in-person staff retreats once or twice a year. Smart managers will react intuitively to their own virtual teams and design ways for them to receive the amount of in-person interaction they want and need.

Guidelines for Success

People aren't perfect, and work situations are rarely perfect, either. Virtual work arrangements may have flaws, and will surely suffer a hiccup or two, but with time and intent, they can be extraordinarily successful. Following a few guidelines for making sure this custom-fit option is successfully implemented will make life easier for everyone involved:

- Be realistic but open-minded about virtual work's limits and opportunities.
- Adopt a performance-based management style.

- Change your leadership style to suit virtual work.
- Design fair and consistent guidelines.
- Set and maintain clear work-life boundaries.

Realistic but Open-Minded

Be realistic but open-minded about virtual work's limits and opportunities. Examine whether a job is a good fit for virtual work. The examples in this chapter make it clear that virtual work is great for those whose main job is to interact with customers or third parties over the phone (making an airline, hotel, or other travel reservation, for example, or filling an order for mail-order products, or selling insurance) or e-mail (collecting sales data from salespeople in the field to aggregate and analyze). Virtual work is easy to adopt for journalists, writers, professors, and other knowledge workers; it's also a natural fit for online organizations like MoveOn and MomsRising. Engineers and computer programmers, who would be working mostly on computer screens even if they were on site, are prime candidates for virtual work. Creative jobs that require solitude and concentration are also ideal for this work arrangement.

Some jobs and careers, however, will always be ill-suited to virtual work. A doctor will need to be present to perform surgery on your knee, and a plumber will always require access to your house to fix your pipes (though one virtually inclined plumber arrived at Nanette's house to replace a leaking faucet with a cell phone in hand to photograph her fixtures, and then proceeded to match them with possible replacements at the hardware store and send photos of new fixtures back to her for approval). But we caution managers not to write off jobs too quickly as fundamentally incompatible. For example, while the surgeon needs to be in the same room with you, some doctors already do diagnosis remotely using video. Nationwide, health information lines have successfully gone virtual, too. Hourly workers and union workers may also find some good fits, depending on the scope of their jobs.

Performance-Based Management

Adopt a performance-based management style. Virtual work is well-suited to performance-based management, a system of review that emphasizes the quality of the work product and meeting clearly defined goals and objectives, not the amount of time an employee spends with managers or coworkers. Performance-based management requires a philosophical shift that can be challenging for managers used to supervising employees by looking over their shoulders and engaging in ad hoc conversations in the hall. Managers of virtual employees simply cannot gauge performance and commitment by checking whose car is still in the parking lot after the close of business. Ed Houghton, director of work-life effectiveness for Pitney Bowes, addresses this common concern among human resources managers by pointing out that because companies routinely demand flexibility of employees, they should reciprocate with flexibility in management style, evaluating employees on their results, just like CEOs.[20] Some human resources professionals suggest training for managers to help them feel more comfortable and proficient in results-based management and to smooth transitions to virtual work.

New Leadership Style

Change your leadership style to suit virtual work. For managers whose reservations about virtual work arrangements stem from apprehension about their ability to change their own leadership style to match the technology, there's help. While there are a variety of virtual work environments, with different methods for meeting business goals, an emerging set of best leadership practices can help ease the transition to remote work, enhancing the manager-employee relationship.

Billie Williamson, a partner at Ernst & Young who oversees the company's diversity programs and has managed virtual teams for more than ten years, offered tips in a *BusinessWeek* report for managing virtual workers. Here are some highlights:

- *Remember that virtual work still involves real people.* It is the manager's responsibility to ensure that relationships among workers and between workers and managers remain vital, that productivity and output are high, and that each team member's contributions are recognized and valued.

- *Use technology in innovative ways to promote team building.* Go beyond the basics of phone and e-mail in order to help create a close group and help workers connect. Set up a community home space with pictures and profiles of team members to help replicate an office atmosphere, or implement a discussion board, a team calendar, and perhaps a chat room.

- *Step up the frequency of communication and check in more often.* This can mean sending e-mail after every phone conference to confirm the action plan and ensure everyone is on board. Meet in person occasionally and, if possible, use videoconferencing. Also, pay attention to silence. Silence can signal consent to a decision, or it can mean the person disagrees with the team's strategy and won't speak up or is simply disengaged. If a team member appears disconnected, begins missing deadlines, or participates less frequently than usual, that's the manager's cue to follow up.

- *Show respect.* This means being sensitive to members who speak English as a second language and paying attention to language and cultural differences and how they shape business protocols. Equalize how you handle differing time zones of global team members instead of insisting on them conforming to your schedule. If regular phone calls at a convenient time for everyone are not possible, shift the start time so that people alternate taking calls during their early morning or late evening hours.[21]

For a manager, it also pays to stay attuned to the individual personalities of virtual workers in order to make sure they succeed. In 2006, the technology company Cisco commissioned a study run by psychologist Stuart Duff to help its managers understand their own virtual workers and the end users of their products. To their surprise, the research showed that the best virtual workers were both highly organized and highly extroverted. Duff had assumed that left-brained introverts would be the most successful working remotely, but instead found that the "life of the break-room party" types thrive in a virtual environment because "left on their own, these types of workers are the ones who work closely with clients, chum around with colleagues, and talk it up to bosses. They stay connected no matter where they are. It comes naturally to them." This means managers may need to use different strategies with different personality types. Based on the study, Cisco executives changed their thinking regarding managing virtual workers and paid more attention to workers who seemed out of the loop. Using videoconferencing instead of relying solely on telephone calls is a method they now use to help every virtual worker succeed, and partnering remote workers with colleagues in their area is another. Some studies assert that only 7 percent of intended meaning is related through solely e-mail interaction. Virtual communication requires managers (and workers) to work hard to replicate what we easily glean from facial expressions, tone of voice, body language, and more.

Fairness and Consistency

Design fair and consistent guidelines. Our research found that designing fair and consistent guidelines for virtual work arrangements works well for companies implementing large-scale virtual work programs or taking entire teams virtual. These guidelines can also provide an excellent metric for workers. A worker interested in a virtual arrangement can first check the company guidelines and determine whether or not there's a chance of approval.

In designing its virtual work program, Blue Cross Blue Shield of Massachusetts formulated a flexible work arrangement worksheet to help managers evaluate individual positions for compatibility with a virtual arrangement. The worksheet includes a contract between the employee and the manager regarding expectations of job performance and productivity. Here are some of the requirements BCBSMA sets forth for workers applying for virtual work arrangements:

- A minimum of three months' continuous regular employment
- Performance that meets or exceeds expectations
- Employee in good standing, and not on any type of corrective action plan
- Position eligible (based on business need) for a virtual arrangement
- Completion of all required privacy, compliance, and security training requirements, as well as online and departmental training as needed
- Completion of leader/associate training that provides tools and skills to be successful in a virtual work arrangement

Yet even without formal guidelines such as these, managers and employees should work together on a case-by-case basis to make virtual work available to those who need and want it. Even allowing workers to connect virtually one or two days a week or to work from home during projects that require intense concentration and focus can go a long way toward increasing productivity and balancing lives on the part of workers.

Clear Work-Life Boundaries

Set and maintain clear work-life boundaries. It is a wonderful thing that 24/7 technology has enabled virtual work to become a reality, but this total accessibility can be used for good—or for evil. In this case, the evil is your work-life balance tipping in the *wrong* direction. Flexibility means for many that work and home life are much more blurred. This can be good for work—in the sense that you don't think twice about responding to e-mail during the weekends or evenings—but bad for family, in the sense that you don't think twice about responding to e-mail during the weekends or evenings! Because work is often done on a more project-driven basis, rather than between the hours of nine and five, both managers of virtual workers and remote employees need to set and respect clearly defined work-life boundaries.

For some, this can mean keeping a space reserved entirely for work; if you're not in your office (wherever it is) you're not on the job. (This can be necessary anyway for virtual customer service representatives who can't have barking dogs or yelling kids in the background.) John Halamka, the CIO for Beth Israel Hospital in Massachusetts, found that integrating the phone lines between the company and off-site locations worked well for employees. Not only did it keep their personal cell phones from being inundated with business calls, it encouraged on-site workers to get over a feeling that they were somehow improperly bothering remote workers by calling them at home. By dialing a five-digit extension to get in touch with virtual colleagues, they felt like their coworkers were just down the hall.

JetBlue gives the control over work-life balance to its workers, as virtual workers are allowed to trade shifts or take voluntary time off or take overtime on the fly. But as discussed in Chapter Two, other companies have exploited flexibility, expecting employees to be available anytime, anywhere. As we explore and make adjustments to virtual work, we all need to ensure that technological innovation doesn't become oppressive, but instead frees us to live and work smarter.

The Wave of the Future

On January 8, 2009, President-elect Obama spoke to the American public about his ideas for an economic stimulus to remedy a deepening recession. Some of the measures contained in the subsequent legislation, the American Recovery and Reinvestment Plan, were infrastructure improvements that would put Americans to work repairing roads, bridges, and schools. If these were reminiscent of New Deal policies, other policies promoted a country of the future, including incentives for the private sector to ramp up production of solar panels and wind turbines and expand broadband lines across the country "so that a small business in a rural town can connect and compete with their counterparts anywhere in the world."

Ready or not, that need to connect and compete, no matter where you are, has already made virtual work a reality. It's the direction our globalized economy is taking us. It's the direction our family structures are taking us. It's the direction businesses are taking us, businesses that want to cut costs and retain talented workers. And it's the direction workers are taking us, workers who want a little more control and a workday that is a lot more sane. In all, we feel it's safe to say that virtual work is well on the way to becoming a centerpiece of the twenty-first-century economy.

5

OFF-RAMPS AND ON-RAMPS

Job and Career Lane Changes

Naima was finance manager at a start-up Internet retailer that had established its niche. After leaving the buttoned-up atmosphere of a large auditing firm, she found the electricity and excitement of the successful start-up infectious and alluring. The work involved frequent long hours and intense deadlines, but it was stimulating and paid well with salary and stock options. Naima took eight weeks off when her first child, a girl, was born, then started her daughter in day care and went back to work. Before she returned, she had negotiated a part-time schedule with her immediate boss, whom she found to be very supportive of her choice to work reduced hours. But after a couple of years, pregnant with her second child, Naima was growing worried about how having two children would affect her career.

She found out when she received her performance review. Though her work was excellent, singled out for praise by the CEO, her review was not; the low ranking on her review did not reflect her performance, but instead a bias against part-time workers. The low ranking meant Naima was not eligible for a stock grant, one of the primary financial bonuses at the company. "I had no choice," her direct manager confessed. "Because you work part-time I *couldn't* give you a better review. I did the best I could." Naima was crushed. Though her manager had worked with her to find a flexible schedule that fit, company policy was clear: working anything less than full time (plus) spelled career death. This point of view was further solidified when one of Naima's colleagues, who had also asked to work a part-time schedule, was denied. Faced with a schedule that fit, but that came with a financial penalty that wasn't commensurate and a corporate culture that didn't value her, Naima declined to return from her second maternity leave.

After seven years of growing with the company, Naima says, "It was so hard to leave. I was there from the beginning when it was all hands on deck." She had truly loved her job. Her boss, on the other hand, told her he wasn't surprised she didn't return. With two kids to care for, he knew she wouldn't come back. "That made me even angrier," she said, "that he said it was because of the kids when I felt I was given no choice."

Now Naima's youngest is in preschool. Because her husband works in real estate, 2009 was a grim reminder that they needed the financial security of two jobs. Besides, Naima found herself itching to flex her career muscle once again. She had found interim work in her years at home doing project-based bookkeeping, but the flexible, at-home work she began with started to creep: more hours and requests to drive into the office. So she began sending her solid and impressive résumé out "into the void," pointedly avoiding the company that had made her choose between career and family in the first place. Yet after nearly a year of trying to get back to work, she still finds herself defending that gap in her résumé as if she had been in jail instead of at home raising children. Her only call-backs have been for full-time positions with overtime and a substantial commute, a schedule that she knows won't work for her family. Still, she feels nervous about turning those down. "My confidence is shaken," she says. "I've been out of the job force and I've lost those business connections."

Naima has reason to be concerned. For parents who can afford it, taking time off work to care for a new child is a wonderful thing, but it tends to have repercussions that profoundly impact future earnings and may make returning to work more difficult than many people realize. Women who take two or three years off on average have earnings that are 20 to 30 percent lower than those of their peers—and they never catch up over the course of their work life. Bias against mothers in hiring, wages, and advancement is well-documented. Job applicants that are identified as mothers are 79 percent less likely to be offered a job.[1] No doubt we will soon hear of studies documenting the economic price of fatherhood, too.

Reentering the job market after caring for a child—or after caring for a parent, another common reason people leave the workforce—is unreasonably difficult for many workers. And, as research has aptly pointed out, the majority of women who take time away from a career *do* want back in eventually—93 percent of them, according to the Center for Work-Life Policy.[2] Ninety-five percent of women in that study also reported they would *not* return to the same employer. It's safe to infer that inadequate workplace support factored in to those decisions, decisions that look a lot like the one Naima made.

Whether pulled out of work to care for children or elderly parents, or sidelined from a lack of mentors or support and networks, workers today are following career trajectories that are decidedly nonlinear. Commonly referred to as "off-ramping and on-ramping," or more recently "sequencing," dipping in and out of the paid or full-time workforce to accommodate life changes is a career model that many of us recognize. In place of the traditional stepladder to success, *Mass Career Customization* authors Cathleen Benko and Ann Weisberg assert, "Increasingly, the career journey of many employees in the knowledge-driven organizations of the twenty-first century will look similar to a sine wave of sorts, with climbing and falling in phases."[3] While some of these workers will want or need to stop work entirely for some period of time, others, like Naima, would prefer not to off-ramp entirely but just downshift a little in the face of growing outside responsibilities and then ramp back up as pressures lessen. Instead of funneling any employee who needs to downshift toward a career dead end, wise leaders will anticipate lane changes and collaborate with employees to find custom-fit solutions.

Involuntary Exits Hurt Businesses

Doug, a high-level manager in a software company, is honest about how roadblocks to employees like Naima emerge. He says that while he "values people having rich lives that are not entirely comprised of work," in the end it was easier for him not to have to make accommodations for employees beyond what would be required by human resources. "I would certainly take into consideration needs like family responsibilities, but to make special arrangements for one employee might cause half my team to ask for special arrangements and we're just not set up to work that way. It may sound cold, but I have a line of qualified engineers waiting to work for me. I don't have any incentive to bend over backward for any individual employee."

Doug's reasoning, while understandable in certain terms, is also short-sighted. Doug feels no incentive to change his managerial style, but his employer has many. Turnover is costly—with estimates ranging from 1.5 to 5 times the high-level employee's salary. For Doug's company, the cost to replace an engineer falls in the solid six figures.

Hema Krishnan, associate dean of the Williams College of Business at Xavier University in Cincinnati, found in a three-year study that though women have ascended the top ranks of businesses in large numbers, the turnover rate of top female executives is almost twice that of male executives. In fields like marketing, operations, and law, the turnover is upwards of 50 percent. Yet these are the very same women—including those with degrees in research and engineering who might work with Doug—who "are perceived very favorably in the business community and, consequently, are likely to be aggressively wooed by other companies and institutions."[4] Forcing women out reduces the diversity of the workplace and removes some of the most highly trained and sought-after workers from the talent pool. And—as the study that found 95 percent of women looking to reenter the workforce reporting they would *not* return to the same employer indicates—forcing women out potentially pushes them into the arms of competitors.

WOMEN LEADERS PRODUCE BUSINESS RESULTS

Studies show that companies with women in leadership are relatively more successful in tough economic environments. A 2008 Pepperdine University study revealed that Fortune 500 companies that had higher numbers of women in upper management outperformed industry medians on key fiscal measures; profits as a percent of revenue were 15 percent higher, profits as a percent of assets were 32 percent higher, and profits as a percent of equity were 31 percent higher.[5]

Krishnan is emphatic about the problem. "This turnover should be of grave concern to companies because an exodus from the corporate suite can have an adverse impact on business performance. It can lead to low morale among rank-and-file employees, loss of valuable human talent, and a perception in the business community that the culture in these companies is dysfunctional." Interviewed in the *New York Times*, Merrill Lynch's director of global diversity and inclusion states clearly that reducing involuntary exits and supporting reentry is not "about paying lip service" but about retaining and recruiting talent and enhancing the bottom line.[6] For Merrill Lynch, staying relevant in the marketplace means retaining women at top levels.

It is not just the realm of high finance that is losing talent. According to the National Center for Education Statistics, though the relative numbers of women faculty have grown, the percentage of tenured women in colleges and universities has remained constant. More women earning doctorates has not translated into more women with good jobs as tenured professors. The differences in salary between men and women professors have actually increased, with more women employed in community colleges, small liberal arts colleges, and at lower academic ranks. The result, according to John W. Curtis, director of research at the American Association of University Professors, is the loss of a strategic edge in attracting the most qualified faculty on the part of academic institutions. "Colleges and universities invest enormous resources to train, hire, and support early-career faculty. By establishing a climate that helps those faculty members succeed, institutions save themselves the costs—both monetary and programmatic—of recruiting new faculty."[7]

Curtis's last point is applicable not just to academia but to all workplaces, and it is here that we cannot place enough emphasis: the change required is as much cultural as it is structural. American workers will not stop having children, taking care of their aging parents, or experiencing health issues—to name just a few of life's events, all of which can make it necessary to temporarily shift priorities. Smart employers will move from a reactive to a proactive model, in which a reduction in a worker's availability is managed successfully and in such a way that it smoothes the worker's nearly inevitable reentry.

How Can Organizations Reduce Exits and Smooth Reentries?

While there is no single answer to the question of reducing the impact of career sequencing, businesses have three successful strategies to consider for workers who need to off-ramp for at least some period of time. Some keep highly trained workers and key employees engaged and connected during the time they take out of the full-time paid workforce, while others ease off-ramped workers back into the fold. And some organizations are creating new career trajectories altogether, in what we call "intelligent redesign": offering an alternative to the traditional up-or-out career path in fields such as law, accounting, and academia.

TIME OFF TO POWER BACK UP

An off ramp can sometimes take the form of a pit stop. Stefan, a designer with a busy New York studio, has taken great pains to counter burnout and replenish his creativity. Every seven years, Stefan changes his voicemail to ask clients to call back in a year, closes down his office, and then spends the next twelve months on personal time, rejuvenating. During the most recent Technology, Entertainment, Design (TED) conference, a prestigious gathering that draws the best and the brightest innovative minds, Stefan presented this simple, yet revolutionary, idea, which allows for his development as a human being and the operation of a thriving business.[8]

Shouldn't we all be so lucky, you might be thinking. Well, maybe we should. Because though the concept of the sabbatical has long been used in the education community, earned by tenured professors who need uninterrupted time to cogitate and do research, many large corporations—about 27 percent of those with more than one thousand employees—use sabbaticals as a perk to retain coveted employees and as an enticement to attract top talent. This group includes technical firms Intel, Microsoft, Silicon Graphics, Adobe Systems, and 3Com.[9] But generally the U.S. record with taking time off is so dismal that the Center for Economic and Policy Research calls us the "No Vacation Nation." And though we're always working, those fun-loving Europeans are at least as productive, if not more so, according to the World Economic Forum. Therefore, even though the idea of regular sabbaticals is a little out of the mainstream for most, time to downshift or take time for self-care—be that learning to snorkel or attending to a health condition—would in fact prove beneficial for us all, businesses included.

Staying Connected

Imagine for a moment a different scenario for Naima. Instead of having her manager dismiss her with "I knew you'd leave" as she quit with regret, assume instead that he understood her need to take a year or so off to focus on her family, but that he anticipated her return. To encourage her to do so, and to bring her talent, knowledge, training, and loyalty back to the company, imagine he assigned her a mentor at the company and offered to pay to keep her license up to date. Before her official return, she could do contract work for the company, as long as she kept it as her only client. Would Naima be searching for a new job now if that had been the case?

Accounting firm Deloitte & Touche bets the answer is no, and has sought to stay connected to workers who resign to care for children or aging parents. In addition to receiving help staying certified, workers in Deloitte's Personal Pursuits Program also have access to the firm's learning and virtual learning centers and are aided in maintaining their business networks.[10]

The Personal Pursuits Program encountered some obstacles. Former employees initially had trouble gaining access to the company intranet, and it took cross-departmental initiative to find a solution. Now, however, the program is cost-effective, helps recruit top talent, and recoups an estimated $150,000 in costs for each employee who returns. Even if they don't return, Senior Manager Julie Keeney says, the program is worth it. "Hopefully they retain a positive sense about the firm, and even if they don't come back to us for whatever reason, they still will be loyal alumni, and that's always a really good thing to have."[11]

Deloitte is just one of a growing number of companies— including Ernst & Young and Merrill Lynch—that are working to retain strong relationships with workers who have off-ramped. Programs like theirs do well when they set up a few basic requirements. For instance, mediocre employees do not make good prospects; to become participants, employees must have performed at the satisfactory level or higher. They also must express a sincere desire to return. And the programs often aren't everlasting; rather, participants should return within one to five years. In return, programs like Deloitte's pay for continuing education or to maintain professional memberships or licenses. Participants should be assigned in-company mentors, and if possible be signed on for contract work during their absence.

Reeling the Talent Back In

When Naima wanted to reenter the workforce after several years spent caring for her children, she had to defend the gap in her résumé. Fortunately, however, more and more companies are attracted to on-rampers like her, seeing the value in their experience and putting resources into pursuing them. Some companies have even rolled out innovative programs that go beyond individual accommodation to create and maintain a business culture that isn't afraid of time spent out of the workforce, and possibly even commends it as a way to produce a well-rounded employee. One on-ramper profiled in the *New York Times* found herself in Naima's position, defending years spent at home. The disconnect between talented workers who want back in, especially women, and the companies that might hire them is puzzling to her. "Most firms have a diversity office," she told the reporter. "Why don't they have an on-ramping department?"[12]

Until the day that becomes a reality, helping to fill the gap are events like a three-day seminar at Columbia University hosted by Merrill Lynch in which thirty-seven off-ramped, formerly high-level women were invited to take part. Over the course of the seminar, the women networked, established mentor relationships, and met with business executives from leading-edge companies like Ernst & Young, Intel, and KPMG. They also gained skills aimed at smoothing their reentry—covering subjects such as how to market themselves and what to expect from a hiring process. All participating companies, including the host, saw the intellectual power behind these women who had stepped off the ladder and wanted to be considered favorably when the women decided to continue their careers.[13]

Coaches and consultants can also provide a helpful salve for the jolt of returning to work after time away. Businesses that do so as part of a parental leave return-to-work program find happier, better adjusted workers with better integration skills. A recent study at the Norwegian University of Life Sciences found that stress was reduced by up to 47 percent for participating workers, with nearly three-quarters saying coaching helped them learn to prioritize their time better and the vast majority—85 percent— expressing that coaching made a significant impact on the management of their day-to-day lives.[14]

Recognizing the cognitive and practical shift required when an employee returns to the workforce after a year or so away, Goldman Sachs created an innovative program that deals with this shift in a very hands-on way. An outgrowth of the New Directions conference—a biannual one-day event offering coaching and guidance—the Goldman Sachs pilot Returnship program is a full-time eight-week reentry boot camp of sorts. People who want to on-ramp work on projects within the firm, whether or not they worked there before they left their careers. Not only does this give managers an excellent opportunity to assess the participants' skills, it also allows people to decide if workforce reentry, or reentry at this level, is right for them on a practical rather than theoretical level. Additionally, the participants were provided training in promoting themselves and their work history and crafting résumés, and they were paired with mentors from the Goldman Sachs Women's Network. After the initial session, Goldman Sachs made offers to more than half of the participants and hopes to expand the program to Hong Kong. Even women who did not receive or seek offers left feeling more confident and better able to navigate a return to paid work.[15]

Intelligent Redesign—Adjusting the Career Track

Offering reentry training or "returnships" and providing additional support for workers coming back from leave are effective ways to help talented workers on-ramp. For some workers, however, there is the added pressure of a deadline for promotion, where the culture of the profession dictates up, out, or off to the side. Attorneys and academics are two groups of professionals that usually face an unwavering schedule for making partner or earning tenure. To take time out for caregiving in the middle of that stretch often results in a permanent departure from the tenure or partner track. Women in particular have a high incidence of getting squeezed out during this period. Further, high-powered business management ladders may not have the same formalized time constraints as law firms and universities, but they nonetheless have rigid and typically unwritten career track expectations that take a heavy toll. Once again, women in particular are being lost on the way up. Some organizations have taken steps to intelligently redesign their career tracks so that individuals can transparently plan their career path. When done well, careers are merely equitably slowed rather than derailed. This has been described as career customization. Deloitte's Corporate Lattice™ is the best-known model program of this kind. It allows managers some choice over their responsibilities as well as their hours and is explicitly intended to keep talented workers on track.

In an article about women off-ramping from science careers, bio-organic chemistry Ph.D. Sarah Webb asks, "In a career where productivity and publications define your value, can you take a couple of years off and then make a successful return? When you do, will employers trust your dedication to your job?"[16] Webb went on to profile four women scientists for whom the answer was yes, yet for whom "successful return" was bittersweet; not one of them ended up with a tenure-track faculty position. One woman Webb profiled, a physicist named Shireen, found independence and flexibility in establishing her own research program, but she also "missed having real start-up money, her own equipment, and the institutional investment that comes with a tenure-track position." Shireen landed on her feet, but she lost—and her university lost—when the institution failed to redesign a career path.

Universities and colleges are beginning to expand their tool-kits to avert this brain drain and retain these employees. Fern, a linguistics professor at an East Coast university, took a semester off from teaching when she had her daughter, and she will come up for tenure one year later than scheduled. If she has another child, the tenure clock will be stopped for one more year. The University of California, Berkeley, has a similar model, designed to ease the tenure crunch. Its intelligent redesign of the track to tenure has four cornerstones:

- Active-service modified duties (ASMD)
- Paid leave
- Tenure clock extension
- A formal commitment to implementing the first three cornerstones[17]

ASMD allows the primary caregiver a reduction of normal duties to prepare or care for a newborn or a foster or adopted child under the age of five. Faculty are eligible from three months prior to giving birth (or adopting a child) to twelve months after the child comes home. Non-birth mothers and fathers can take advantage of the program for one semester; birth mothers up to two semesters in addition to six weeks of paid childbearing leave and the option of unpaid leave for a term of up to one year. And, with an option similar to the one offered to Fern, U.C. Berkeley allows anyone who has caregiving responsibilities to stop the tenure clock for up to two years (an option, it should be noted, that helps professors while costing the university little). So what does this look like in practice? It usually equates to having to teach fewer classes or even a temporary cessation of teaching responsibilities, without having to "make up" one's own classes in subsequent semesters. Perhaps more important, faculty who take advantage of the program are not punished for the slowdown the way Naima was at her company.

The University of California has not only developed these policies and conducted research on the need and ramifications of them, it has developed an initiative—the UC Faculty Family Friendly Edge—that mandates the implementation of these policies for the good of the most prestigious state university system in the country. The executive summary of the toolkit outlining the policies boldly declares that in taking action more than just the faculty are served: "For the University to retain its world class reputation, all faculty members must have equal opportunities to be productive contributors throughout the course of their careers. Family friendly departments are essential to the continued vitality of the University of California."[18]

ON-RAMP PROGRAMS HELP LANE CHANGERS

Good news for those reentering the workforce: the number of programs designed to help workers with on-ramping is growing. Between 2004 and 2008, when the term and topic began to take off in the media and receive attention, fifty-seven programs were launched. Since then five more programs have been added, according to iRelaunch's "Comprehensive List of Career Entry Programs Worldwide." These include programs offered around the globe at universities, companies, government agencies, professional associations, and foundations.[19]

Helpful as they are, it doesn't take structured programs or policies to adjust the career-track expectations of workers facing down a tenure clock or partnership deadline who have other responsibilities. Cindy, the attorney introduced in Chapter Three who negotiated a reduced workload at her firm while she raised two kids, initially encountered an obstacle much like the one Naima faced. While they allowed her to work part time, her firm made it clear that they will not offer partnership to part-time employees. Cindy has fought back. While another associate may only bring in 50 percent of what they bill (often hours are lowered if they seem excessive for the project, and sometimes money isn't recovered from clients), Cindy has a realization rate of over 90 percent. When she argued this fact—her business worth—to the firm, the management compromised on a solution. Though partnership isn't available to her, they agreed that "of counsel" designation is, a status that is as respectable as partner, and that previously wasn't available as a way to promote associates. Cindy appreciates her firm's efforts, and says she is unlikely to switch to a firm that is less supportive of her desire for work-life fit.

Negotiating mutually beneficial arrangements for workers facing an off-ramp situation is both possible and ideal. In Cindy's case, it allowed her and her husband to avoid child-care costs and to spend ample time with their kids. From the firm's point of view, it not only retained an associate whose hourly billing rate to clients has increased over the years, it has produced an unexpected benefit (one that we've seen time after time when employers accommodate work-life needs): the arrangement actually helps in building relationships with clients. "Clients appreciate the flexibility, and hearing and seeing that our firm is amenable to all types of people. And it's pretty clear that not just parents need flexibility. We have people who are taking care of their parents, or who have medical problems, or who have other commitments in the community. I see it as a win-win for the firm, for our clients, and for potential clients, too, because work is really trending towards this flexible, customizable, realistic approach," says Cindy. In fact, the benefits her firm reaps are part of the reason Cindy thinks the situation is still working so well, even though the economy is much harsher than it was when Cindy first started working part time.

How Workers Can Smooth Their On-Ramps

While employers bear responsibility for putting together toolkits and supporting their use, creating departments, programs, or mentoring systems to help ease transitions, workers returning to the job market after a period away must also do what they can to make their return as easy as possible. Just as Cindy worked hard to negotiate her own creative solution within her firm, as an off-ramped worker you can help yourself succeed in a variety of ways, from doing meaningful and challenging volunteer work (and putting it on your résumé) during time away from the paid labor force to staying current in your field.[20]

Managers offer this advice to off-ramped or on-ramping workers:

- *Keep in touch with former coworkers and managers:*

  Keeping in touch doesn't mean years of having the same conversation, or offering the same transparent lunch invitation, to people you hardly knew during your workdays. Rather, it's about taking the time to nurture genuine friendships that may have budded in the workplace. For colleagues with whom you had less of a personal connection, it may mean continuing the friendship through social and professional networking sites.[21]

- *Keep your skills current, including staying on top of technological advances, business literature, and market trends:*

  If your company subscribed to a trade publication, purchase your own subscription and continue reading it. If the trends in your business can be tracked through publications like the *Wall Street Journal*, again, a subscription is worth the cost. Today there are free news aggregating services on the Internet that you can subscribe to for different fields. Find one that's right for you and read it when it arrives in your e-mail inbox. When you are ready to return to the workplace, you will be able to offer informed opinions on the transitions the business has encountered while you've been away, an important component for any interview or networking event.

- *Attend professional conferences and workshops to improve your industry knowledge:*

   Like keeping up on trade publications, attending conferences is an effective way to stay abreast of the latest industry trends. You'll be well-informed about what changing needs and expectations exist in your field, and where and how you can slide back in when you're ready to return to the workforce.

- *Do volunteer work that affects an organization's bottom line or enhances your leadership skills:*

   Whether you're an accountant, a marketer, a salesperson, or in any of a number of other professions, volunteer work might involve contributing your time and skills to a charity. Or it might mean becoming involved with a start-up or a fledgling organization that needs some expert advice. Lacey, a lawyer for a large Arizona firm, took several years off work to care for her children, but offered her legal skills during political elections. Though her husband worked a demanding job with extreme hours, he knew well in advance that he would need to take time off when election days rolled around. Lacey was able to keep her mind sharp, contribute to her community in a meaningful way, and create an experience to share when she reentered the workforce.

HOURLY WORKERS: OFF-RAMPS CAN HURT

Without the opportunity to adjust one's hours of work, hard-won economic gains can be set back by a joyous event—a child's birth—as well as by a sad one—a spouse's major illness. Especially vulnerable are hourly workers. According to the Center for Law and Social Policy (CLASP), a national nonprofit organization that advocates for policies to improve the lives of low-income people, few initiatives reach the lower-paid hourly workers who have the least flexibility and security at work, the least ability to pay for help, and the least ability to afford missing pay. For these workers, exiting the paid workforce to care for a relative isn't just a bittersweet event or a career stopper—it's a catastrophe. Employers would do well to consider the needs of hourly workers and make efforts to retain them. One solution is to offer, when possible, some paid family leave, particularly for the care of a newborn or critically ill relative.

- *Take continuing education classes to refresh skills, or to learn new ones:*

    According to the U.S. Department of Education, more and more workers are looking to associate's degrees and certificate programs for reentry training, with a 28 percent increase of sub-baccalaureate awards being granted between 1997 and 2007.

Elizabeth, for example, was a news anchor and reporter at TV stations across the country. Though she never completely left the workforce, after her son's birth her career shifted dramatically: first she worked occasionally at the TV station as a freelancer, then took a weekend job at a news radio station, then moved into doing part-time work for an audiobook production company and did occasional voice-over work. "As my son grew older and more independent, I felt a growing sense of dissatisfaction," she said. "I wanted to get back to work, but I didn't want to go back to news," having found the job too difficult to do meaningfully on a part-time basis. So Elizabeth shifted gears completely. Enticed by the potential benefits of flexible hours and telecommuting in freelance writing and editing, Elizabeth enrolled in a certificate course at the local university. Though she says she learned a lot from the program, there were additional benefits that Elizabeth didn't anticipate as she shifted to her new custom-fit career, including opportunities to try out different types of projects to decide what she enjoyed and was good at, as well as a chance for a hands-on internship. Elizabeth's experience yields tips for off-ramped workers—parents especially—who decide to use continuing education to find a port of reentry:

- If you enroll in a certificate program, make a point of getting to know the instructors. They can provide confidence-boosting encouragement, résumé advice, and internship opportunities.

- Make your own opportunities. As part of the certificate program, a number of working professionals came in and spoke to the class about their jobs. But when Elizabeth sat down to think about it, the kind of job that sounded most interesting to her was the one that her instructor had. At the last class, she asked the instructor if her company ever took on interns. The instructor said they had never had an intern before, but after talking it over with her colleagues, they created an internship for Elizabeth.

- Take an internship, even if it seems ridiculous to do so at your age. In addition to gaining hands-on experience, internships, like the Goldman Sachs Returnship program, can lead to job offers within the company or leads to positions at other companies.

- Make business cards. When Elizabeth first had hers printed, she showed them to everyone. You don't have to ask people for jobs or be pushy. Someone would say, "How are you?" And Elizabeth would say, "Great! I just got new business cards. Would you like to see?" She was amazed at how many friends and acquaintances told her about potential jobs.

- Sign up for social networking sites. One of the students in Elizabeth's certificate program started a Facebook group for people in the program, where people could post job listings they heard about. The class also has a LinkedIn group.

Enrolling in continuing education programs and community college courses is an excellent way to on-ramp after time away from the paid workforce and to acquire new skills when any type of lane change requires them.

Merging a Workforce of Lane Changers

All custom-fit arrangements are based on an understanding—indeed, a workplace culture—that a worker is a whole person. When a company values the human capital of people who have breaks in their résumés, they facilitate on-ramping and attract workers with valuable, productive talent. It also means starting the conversation before a worker is ready to quit. Employers that prioritize the retention of and partnership with valued workers needn't necessarily lose them to the playground, or lose them for long.

Businesses and organizations that will survive in our diverse, globalized business environment are those ready to implement and endorse practices such as ongoing networking, training, and mentoring to attract people who have exited or downshifted at times in their life course. Workers who will successfully negotiate nonlinear career paths are those who make the effort to stay connected and engaged if they off-ramp and who work with their employers to find creative solutions if life and work collide.

Hit the accelerator or hit the brakes: most of us will do both in our lifetimes. As more and more workers compose nonlinear work lives that speed up or slow down for sabbaticals, caregiving, or military or public service, the time has come for businesses and workers—like new teenage drivers—to realize that learning how to merge is a safe way to ensure that everyone thrives.

6

CONTRACT WORK AND ON-DEMAND TALENT

A Fit for Some

We've all seen the ads in the weekly paper: "Earn $$$ in Your Spare Time!" Sure, lots of people would love to get a big paycheck for work done on their own schedule, but very few believe these dubious claims of an easy, lucrative, home-based livelihood. Certainly not Naima, the educated financial manager who wants to reenter the workforce now that her children are more independent. It's fair to say stuffing envelopes will not meet her intellectual and financial needs. Nor will these types of offers catch the attention of Chandra, laid off from her tech job and now finally pursuing that Ph.D. she always dreamed of; nor Jim, an attorney who retired early from his corporate firm to spend time with his wife, who was starting her second round of chemotherapy (but who's now happily in remission).

These are three of the thousands of workers who are out of the paid workforce—pulled or pushed out by caregiving, layoffs, or a conscious choice to leave a rigid or extreme job in order to live a more balanced life. But these three are also workers with energy, talent, education, and experience. A full-time job that stretches the boundaries of fifty or sixty hours a week is not the answer for any of them at this time, yet they all have valuable skills to offer and would eagerly embrace work that met their particular and distinctive needs. Recognizing their availability and understanding their terms, increasingly companies from fledgling start-ups to corporate giants are using contract workers for interim, project-based work that meets the changing demands of business as well as life. While part of the current increase can be attributed to the sagging economy, experts agree—with conflicting feelings—that the trend is not going away.

All indicators point to the fact that companies looking for experienced on-demand workers are finding they have an ever-deepening pool to dip into. On-demand talent that signs on for projects lasting weeks or months makes up about 8 percent of the U.S. workforce, according to Barry Asin, president of Staffing Industry Analysts. This adds up to 10 million Americans in all, with some experts predicting contract jobs will grab an ever-increasing share of the job market in the years to come.[1] And while fifteen years ago contract workers mostly filled in doing office work—remember the Kelly Girl?—now more than half of the positions call for professionals.

Economic downturns appear to only increase the openings for on-demand talent. As we write this in 2010, the still common occurrence of a "reduction in force"—a term layoff targets know well—is contributing to an increase in contract work. According to the latest figures from the Bureau of Labor Statistics, on-demand workers were filling more positions in late 2009 than they had since 2004. Not only are contract workers often the first to be laid off in hard times, they're usually the first to be hired back or hired to replace permanent employees by skittish companies.[2] These types of numbers inspired Gary Mathiason, of the employment law firm Littler, to predict that fully half of jobs created in the economic recovery would go to a contract workforce.[3] A study conducted by the staffing firm Veritude found 45 percent of companies saying they would use temporary workers as part of their current and future workforce, even among companies that laid off contingency workers during the recession.[4]

The breadth of contract work is expansive, and by definition can cover anyone from a field worker to a "permatemp"—a contract worker retained seemingly indefinitely without benefits or options, as in the 1990s' dot-com boom. Indeed, in its darkest variant, companies use contract work as a way to avoid treating workers fairly by extracting their work without offering commensurate pay or benefits, exploiting eager workers for low cost. And while it's true that the difficult economy of 2008–2010 is now trending positive for contract workers, anyone let go from a permanent position and replaced with an on-demand worker instead of being hired back might not see the jobs report as entirely rosy. Indeed, we could write an entire book just on the complicated, and now global, world of contract labor.

In this chapter, we confine our discussion to just one narrow slice of this very large pie: workers, primarily though not exclusively professionals, who have *chosen* to forgo some of the advantages of working on staff for the flexibility and custom fit that contract work, at its best, allows. It is this select form of contract work that has proven resilient in a tough market, and seems increasingly coveted in the custom-fit workplace emerging today.

Matchmakers and SWATS: Making Contracting Connections

In the new landscape of contracting, contract workers are not the only group whose numbers are swelling. If the at-home talent pool and the companies-in-need are like singles looking for the perfect match, firms like Flexperience might be considered their matchmaker. Flexperience, founded by two mothers, is a California company that works to place workers just like Michelle, Chandra, and Jim with local clients in sectors such as high-tech, finance, biotech, and retail. Featured in an *ABC News* story in March 2009—when California's unemployment rate was topping 10 percent—Flexperience finds itself with a full range of skilled professionals looking to be placed in temporary positions to cover a leave of absence, advise on special projects, or help get a company off the ground.[5] Similarly, Business Talent Group, a firm that places executives who choose to do contract work, saw business rise by 70 percent in the second quarter of 2009.[6]

Though the *Economist* falls short of agreeing that firms like these are the wave of the future, it can't argue with their success.

"Call the Business Talent Group (BTG) in Los Angeles or Epoch in Boston, for example, and they will be able to offer you anything from a chief executive to a forensic accountant. If you have more specialized needs you can call Tatum (which specializes in financial executives) or the Nielsen Healthcare Group. The market for executive temps is so buoyant that even old warhorses of recruiting, such as Heidrick & Struggles, are sticking their noses into it."[7] And this trend is not confined to highly trained professionals. LiveOps, a Silicon Valley-based company that does call-center outsourcing, is finding itself struggling to meet demand from both virtual contractors and the clients who want them. The independent contractors it places are able to manage their work on a highly customized level, signing up for half-hour shifts any time of the day or night. Eighty percent of the contract workers it employs are female, and a majority of them either have children at home or are caring for someone with special needs. For workers needing extreme flexibility, this type of situation can be ideal.

While firms that connect at-home workers with interested companies are playing an increasing role in filling this growing niche in customized work arrangements, often the contractors make their own connections. Downsized or off-ramping workers can negotiate terms with former employers for contract work. And with so many people now utilizing this option for work, contractors are forming networks of their own. Christine Heenan has been Harvard University's vice president for government, community, and public affairs, done policy work for the Clinton White House, and headed up government and community relations at Brown University. After having her second child, she rejected an on-staff job and chose instead to consult for Brown. "Two years into that, I hired my first employee who was actually my neighbor, whose background was banking and nonprofits, but was home with her three young children at the time." The next employee of what would become the successful Clarendon Group was also a career professional home with a new child.[8]

In fact, it would appear that increasingly, the parents chatting at the schoolyard gate have experience and education just waiting to be tapped, exactly the scenario described in Chapter Five with those talented off-rampers taking time out of the paid workforce. Mindy Storrie, director of leadership for the University of North Carolina's Kenan-Flagler Business School, told the *Wall Street Journal* the school was able to assemble a team of eight at-home mothers to teach leadership skills to M.B.A. students. Specifically, these moms role-played difficult management situations with the students, then critiqued their performances. The team, assembled by using the same type of neighborhood networking Clarendon used, included a Stanford University neuroscientist, a University of Virginia M.B.A., an attorney, and a news executive. The *Wall Street Journal* calls this phenomenon the "rise of the mommy 'SWAT team'"— where "SWAT" stands for "smart women with available time." They "... assemble quickly through networking and staffing firms to handle crash projects. Employers get lots of voltage, cheap, while the women get a skills update and a taste of the professional challenges they miss."[9]

Who's On Tap?

A talent-on-demand environment that allows workers to be judged not by their age, location, and work history gaps but rather on their skills and experience is a boon for off-ramped stay-at-home parents and semiretired workers alike. It ensures that companies will judge the candidate more on ability to deliver results and less on how those results will be obtained.[10] As Flexperience co-founder Sally Thornton told ABC, "We have tri-athletes and Ph.D.'s and working moms and working dads— there are lots of reasons people want flexibility."[11] Besides parents, the most common on-demand workers include people who are seeking a more balanced life, retirees, and workers who are returning to the workforce after an extended absence.

Worker Seeking Balance

As discussed in Chapter One, the perfect maelstrom of globalization, a 24/7 economy, and the unattainable vision of the ideal worker has struck, and we've all had enough. Many people have simply hit their limit, especially those workers who self-identify as having extreme jobs and are setting limits with the role their work holds in their lives before stress overloads, poor health, or failing personal connections make the decision for them. These workers may want to reduce their stress, ramp up their spiritual or community commitments, or spend more time at home. They are choosing to opt out of the full-time staff position of yesterday for a challenging but more controllable contract position today.

Tom, a forty-eight-year-old father of three, elected to be a contract worker as a way to reorder his priorities. As the manager of a commodity trading group, Tom lived on adrenaline: every day, life was a rush—twelve- to fourteen-hour shifts, monthly flights to Singapore on private jets, power over scores of people and millions of dollars, not to mention a very comfortable living. By age forty-five, Tom was financially secure and at the top of his game. Left out of this equation was his wife, who worked as a nurse, as well as his daughters and his young son. Arriving home well after the kids were in bed, "family time" meant tired conversations with a spouse who was growing weary of life with his paycheck, but without *him*. A move back to the United States from London helped somewhat, but the long hours and responsibility then became compounded by nasty organizational politics, the sludge of a bureaucratic environment, and the growing economic chaos that threatened what had been one of the advantages of his position—the stability and financial security of his job. When the rounds of layoffs finally began, Tom stepped up and offered to go.

"I gave up a steady paycheck and the support and staff of a large organization. What I gained was the freedom to manage my business as I see fit, time with my family, and the ability to watch my teenage children develop." Tom describes leaving his extreme job as a "come to Jesus" moment for him and for his family. Since moving to consulting, Tom has turned down three lucrative full-time job offers that would have meant moves to Europe or work hours that would preclude newfound priorities like coaching his son's baseball team, as he has for the last two years. In choosing project-based work over prestige and power, Tom echoes a sentiment many contract workers express: "Some things are more important than money."

(Almost) Retiree Seeking Challenge and Income

Like Tom, who at forty-eight years of age just meets the Census Bureau's definition of a Baby Boomer, many workers choose contract work later in life after experiencing a degree of professional success. It's impossible to predict exactly what will happen when 70 million Boomers retire from the workforce, though a shortage of some of the most experienced and skilled workers in the labor pool is a reasonable consequence to anticipate— and "likely to create a growing demand for older workers," according to an *Economist* report on the temp agency Manpower.[12] Yet for reasons such as needing additional income to provide for either children or their own elderly parents, Boomers are not willing (or able) to quit the workforce altogether.[13] These highlights from the "New Retirement Survey" conducted by Merrill Lynch and Harris Interactive show some of the compelling reasons why this generation of workers is well suited to on-demand contracting or cycling in and out of paid work:[14]

- While 76 percent of Boomers intend to keep working and earning in retirement, on average they expect to retire at the age of sixty-four and then try out an entirely new job or career.

- Boomers' first-choice retirement plan is to repeatedly cycle between periods of work and leisure (42 percent), followed by part-time work (16 percent).
- Sixty-seven percent of Boomers say they would be motivated to work after retirement for the mental stimulation and challenge.
- Boomers are earnings-motivated and also three times more worried about a major illness (48 percent), their ability to pay for health care (53 percent), or winding up in a nursing home (48 percent), than about dying (17 percent).
- Boomer women are better educated, more independent, and more financially engaged than any generation in history.
- Boomer women see retirement (and an empty nest) as an opportunity for career development and continued personal growth.

No doubt that the Boomers' attitudes, experiences, and work ethic represent an unprecedented opportunity to leverage a tremendously valuable segment of the nation's human capital—even if they can't or don't want to work year-round, full time.

Worker Seeking Test-Drive

Workers who have been out of the workforce for a year or more but contemplate returning might choose on-demand work as a way to test whether they're ready to return. On-demand work can also help them identify the job they want. In this respect, Flexperience, BTG, and other firms of this type offer work as independent contractors as a way to keep off-ramped workers' skills not only up-to-date but developing in terms of breadth and experience. For these on-ramping workers, contract work allows them to vet potential employers as well. Flexperience has allowed workers like Deborah Kopleman, mother of two young kids, to be placed on a six-month project for a biotech company and thus "to try on and experiment with different career opportunities."[15] This arrangement goes both ways: just as workers like Deborah can test-drive companies to make sure they're a good fit, the companies can likewise test out the workers to make sure they're meeting the company's needs. This test-drive period is one of the many reasons why contracting with this skilled work-force is a boon to companies as well.

The Benefit for Businesses

Before posting and hiring for a position, businesses would do well to consider whether the job has to be done full time and on site. Could the job be performed on a part-time or project basis? Or could it be broken in half and performed by two people? If the answers are yes, contract work makes good business sense.

Before delving into the business case, it must be acknowledged that employing contract workers does have a downside for businesses. Employers are unlikely to foster the same degree of loyalty with a contractor that they would with an in-house worker. They may want someone in-house they can develop and grow and invest in long-term, wanting to avoid the project management and training that may be required with a contractor. But often, what a business needs more than anything else is to be nimble and lithe, and contractors are an ideal solution to this need.

Just as with an on-demand product you might enjoy at home—a movie, for example—for businesses, too, there is the instant gratification of having exactly what you need right when you want it. Their very flexibility is a reason contractors are also known as "contingency workers," affording businesses quick, viable options for ramping up to launch a new product, and downsizing quickly if circumstances change. Profiled in both *BusinessWeek* and the *New York Times*, Eggrock, a manufacturer of premade bathrooms, had reduced its factory floor staff by more than three-quarters during hard times. When a large order came in for a hospital project, Eggrock obtained the plumbers, electricians, and assemblers from Manpower, not certain enough in its future to hire back permanent employees.[16]

Additional benefits:

- *Lowered costs.*

    Companies both large and small appreciate the cost savings associated with these workers. Typically contract workers do not carry benefits, are not entitled to paid time off, and because they are not regular employees, their use relieves businesses of the burden of payroll taxes. The ability to hire and fire them on demand spares companies from paying for workers they do not need. Overall, contractors can cost businesses 30 percent less than regular employees. On the other side, changing to a contract situation can be either an excellent or inevitable option for some workers with intense caregiving responsibilities. According to a MetLife survey that looked at full-time employees who are also caregivers, issues such as absenteeism and workplace interruptions cost employers $33.6 billion.[17] The cost savings in shifting the arrangement can serve as a hook for businesses.

    In addition, while fledging companies may not be able to afford a new hire—especially at a top level of a company—they can pay for that expertise for a short time. This is especially useful in legal and finance positions. "Small companies like us because we have part-time CFOs or part-time general counsels, so it's that critical expertise that a startup needs at a rate that they can afford," said Flexperience's Thornton.[18]

- *Market for top talent.*

    Advocates of contracting with executive-level workers argue that the traditional market for managers—and particularly for chief executives—could be best described as inefficient. Companies that follow the traditional model search out-of-house for top-level management personnel to bring in as full-fledged staff members. Yet despite all the effort put into finding and securing these hired guns, one in five of them leave within just eighteen months. Especially if an executive is needed for a strategic reason or to lead a certain project, contracting may make more sense for the business. As one placement firm eloquently put it: "Clients aren't always looking to hire people, but rather a specific person, to be the solution to their problem."[19]

- *Try before you buy.*

Just as contract workers are afforded the opportunity to find an excellent fit in terms of future employment by trying out a range of jobs and companies, hiring contract workers offers businesses the same prospect of finding a relationship that might work in the long term. A quarter of the interim executives placed by BTG have been offered permanent positions.[20]

- *Acquire experienced workers.*

Top-level contract workers bring with them a competitive edge because they already possess the knowledge and expertise they need to do their work. Retirees and off-ramped parents may be familiar with a certain company's internal operations, especially if they've been doing consulting or contract work for their former employer. Expanding both how work is done and the parameters for who might be right for the job, using on-demand talent is one more way in which embracing flexibility broadens the options for today's businesses.

Deciding Whether to Be a Contractor: Benefits and Trade-Offs

Contract work is just one of a wide menu of custom-fit options, and might not be right for everyone. As with every choice, its advantages and drawbacks must be considered in crafting your own custom fit. When you are armed with the information about how contract work lends itself to customization, as well as what you give up with contract work, you can best make the decision about whether it's an option that fits for you. Here are some of the most common considerations:

The variety of assignments available to contractors means you can experience a wide variety of work environments and build breadth in skills and experience. This knowledge then transfers to future on-demand assignments, making you ever more desirable as an on-demand worker and increasing your attractiveness to future long-term employers. On the other hand, those who relish the connection and security of a long-term relationship with both a company and coworkers will find themselves wanting more.

On-ramping employees are well-served by keeping their skills fresh and staying abreast of relevant growth and market trends in their chosen industry through contract work. In addition, employers and colleagues at contract firms form the basis of an excellent network to tap into when you decide to seek a permanent position. In the current economic climate, some experts say that the contractor-turned-employee scenario has become less common, and employers may stay commitment-shy for some time. Contracting with a former employer, however, can be an excellent bridge that replaces a reduction of hours or a job share.

Contract work can offer a lot of control in choosing how and when you work, even the length of your assignments and the intensity of the hours and the job. Unlike a permanent employee, you have a choice not to take assignments while the kids are out of school for the summer, or when you want to take a long vacation. Note, however, that for many workers this control is exchanged for decreased or nonexistent benefits, including health care and retirement plans; a general lack of stability; and not as much choice as one would like for plum jobs (given to permanent employees). On-demand workers who go through an agency should vet the agency carefully and be aware of the placement costs and terms.

Depending on your skills and the industry, both your immediate availability and your relevant skills can translate into excellent pay for your work. Businesses are able to pay more because they save the time and money spent on hiring, training, development, and benefits. On the other hand, some companies and institutions use contract workers because they can pay them less. Universities, for example, are notorious for their use of adjunct faculty to reduce costs. Others have been accused of abusing contract workers by using them essentially as permanent employees but withholding valuable benefits and bonuses.

Permanent employees will typically remain the core of any company, and will be the first to receive continuing education, training, and concentrated career development. Contractors are expected to already possess the skills necessary to do whatever job they were hired to do. Similarly, many organizations try to fill positions internally and promote from within; consequently, the most desirable jobs could stay out of reach.

As one type of custom fit, contract or on-demand work can prove an excellent solution for those who prioritize flexibility over stability. It works particularly well for those who would otherwise remain out of the paid workforce, like retirees or workers with caregiving responsibilities, as well as workers whose expertise is in demand. Additionally, as discussed in Chapter Four, new technology and communication systems have made it easier than ever to work with employees and contractors without requiring them to be at the office. The talent you need may be across the country or globe and you can still access it.

One of the most exciting aspects of on-demand work is the sheer number of people and variety of businesses that can benefit from this arrangement. It works for parents and non-parents alike, stay-at-home caregivers, and chief executives who don't want to be tied to one company for a long period of time. It works for young workers with hot skills (for example, the technical consultants who can set up your Web site and your marketing platforms) as well as for older workers with wisdom and decades of experience in an industry or job. The development of a professional contract workforce is relatively new and seems concomitant to our 24/7 business environment. On-demand workers can address the needs of companies in high-velocity environments, where product cycles are short and competitors are ready to pounce, for those who need expertise *now*. Yet the arrangement is also within reach for young businesses that can't afford the solid-gold offers a permanent CFO or in-house counsel would require. In fact, it is the inherent flexibility of this option for both sides that makes on-demand work such an exciting development in and part of the new custom-fit workplace.

7

WHEN BABIES GO TO WORK

A Simple Solution to a Common Need

What do you need to get you through your workday? Briefcase? Check. BlackBerry? Check. Baby? Check? Even if you are a parent, the very thought of putting "baby" and "office" together evokes disaster scenes for most people—employers and employees alike. After all, isn't that what all the worry about child care and opting-out and nanny cams hidden in teddy bears is about: the necessary separation of work and family?

The idea of bringing infants to work before they reach the crawling stage still meets resistance from a majority of American companies, in part because of our deeply ingrained ideas of what a proper workplace looks and feels like, and our set ideas of who belongs in it. Contemporary American workplaces and culture have evolved (or, we might say, devolved) to a point where there is too often an expectation that a person is either a good worker or a good parent—but that both shouldn't happen in the same place.

But the reason babies-at-work programs are a tough sell isn't because they can't work, says Carla Moquin, founder and president of the Parenting in the Workplace Institute. Rather, the concept itself simply feels foreign. Yet as strange as it may seem to some (including those who wouldn't think twice about bringing a pinball machine or a putting green to a high-tech firm), babies have gone to work with parents since the beginning of human history—on the backs of farm-laboring mothers and even with heads of state like Queen Victoria. And while a working parent has different options for managing the needs of a new baby—taking a leave of absence, switching to contract work, job sharing, and others—sometimes the best option is the simple one.

Despite resistance by managers and employees alike, today formal babies-at-work programs are popping up and—to the delight of scores of new parents—working well. Parents (including a number of fathers) have successfully brought their babies to workplaces ranging from cubicles to retail environments, and from companies with as few as three employees to companies employing more than three thousand. A recent survey by the Parenting in the Workplace Institute found that more than 130 companies—including credit unions, management consulting firms, stores, private schools, and law offices—have instituted formal arrangements to allow parents of infants to bring them to work until the age of six to eight months.[1] These programs are entirely different from employer-supported infant-care options such as on-site day care. They allow parents to perform their regular jobs while wearing, feeding, and watching over the new baby.

While parents-to-be are usually the instigators of these pilot babies-at-work programs, sometimes a manager or human resources staffer does so for one of a number of reasons: a supervisor is worried about losing a key employee following parental leave; a manager is concerned about losing consistency in service to an important client while someone is on leave; a chief executive is worried about losing the human capital of high-performing employees when they off-ramp to care for a new infant but return to work for a competitor down the road. As we've seen again and again throughout our research, when employers recognize the needs of their workers, they win their loyalty. In one study of a babies-at-work program, all participants reported being highly satisfied with their jobs. The mothers (no fathers participated in the study) credited the program with decreasing their stress level, and with decreasing the perception of their absenteeism.[2]

Wherever the idea originates—from an expectant mother, a thoughtful employer, or the readers of concepts like those presented in this book—companies trying out babies-at-work programs have largely found that this accommodation for parents reaps concrete benefits for the company. Improved worker retention? Check. Fewer sick days for babies and parents alike? Check. A sense of community for everyone in the workplace? Check.

Unlike flexible work options that can be used by a range of workers, we recognize that this is a customized work arrangement for a specific point in certain people's lives: when a worker has a new baby. Yet even if you're not an expectant parent, as a coworker or manager you are still a vital part of why this custom-fit option works. Babies-at-work programs help employees excel at their jobs *and* at parenting. The concerns that employers have about allowing babies in the workplace can be addressed, and the program can be implemented successfully in almost any organization.

Parent Versus Worker

The pervasive cultural image of the "ideal worker" is more the guy with the Bluetooth attached to his ear than the guy with his hiking boots stashed in his car, hoping to hit the trail after work. (But either way, it's likely to be a guy—the cultural image hasn't altogether caught up with the culture.) This ideal worker is available 24/7, always "on," ready to put all of life's priorities aside for work. He never thinks about rearranging his schedule to take his son to kung fu class—let alone take a new baby to work—gasp! Never mind that the complete accessibility and single-minded focus of the ideal worker fuels burnout, calcifies gender stereotypes, and encourages some parents to quit or downshift their careers, unaware of the possibility of other options. As discussed in depth in preceding chapters, this expectation has forced sacrifices and hard decisions that leave employed parents torn and unsatisfied and increase the chances they will quit. As a working mother quoted in *Time* magazine captured it, "We live in a society where too many people make workers choose—do you want to be a good parent, or do you want to be a good worker?"[3]

As a result, the expectation of the "ideal worker" has pushed many talented employees who happen to be parents out of the workforce entirely, or into extended leaves, or to more family-friendly professions or corporations, or to entrepreneurship. Many are like Jill, a former editor at a midsized publisher who grew increasingly worried, as she tried to get pregnant, that having a baby would signal a diminished commitment to her job and perhaps even end her career. "My boss told me that when she was at work she was not a parent—there her daughter ceased to exist." To Jill, however, the briefcase and the baby are not antithetical. She sensed she could forge a custom fit, somehow. When she started her family, she decided to leave the publishing house and join a very family-friendly, flexible company. Yet even though it had been founded by two mothers, Jill nonetheless was reluctant to request she bring her baby daughter to work for the first few months. "I thought it would be too distracting," she admits. At that time, Jill didn't know that all she had to do was ask. Her colleagues later said they would have been more than happy to accommodate the request, though they also didn't think to offer the arrangement.

Advocates of babies-at-work programs point out that they are good for everyone—companies and employees. Rather than staying stuck in that tired "parent versus worker" mentality, we need to recognize "good parent equals good worker." This is a paradigm change but one that some thoughtful leaders are already spearheading. That working mother quoted in *Time*, the one who defied the false choice between worker and parent? She is U.S. Secretary of Health and Human Services Kathleen Sebelius. Back then she was Kansas Insurance Commissioner and working mother of two. She took two infant sons to work as the executive director of her state's trial lawyers association. She remains a steadfast advocate of babies-at-work programs.

Good Parent = Good Worker

Many parents, like Jill, return to work in the first weeks or months following childbirth to face expectations and norms that don't fit with the reality of their new lives. What they typically find is described in *The Milk Memos*, a book in which IBM professionals Cate Colburn-Smith and Andrea Serrette detail a first day back at work in both horrifying—and for too many women, familiar—terms:

> There's a parade of well-meaning colleagues welcoming you back and asking you endless questions about the baby, which just makes you miss him all the more. Besides giving the baby report, you'll spend the day trying to refocus your mind on your work, and figuring out when and how to pump. You will count the hours until you can be with your baby again. And you will probably cry.[4]

No one gets anything out of this. Not the company that needs this torn and stressed new parent, not the coworkers who may be concerned for her or annoyed by her changed focus, and certainly not the woman herself—alternately moping, crying, and pumping. (It's no accident there's no father in this scenario. Perhaps no one has even noticed he has a child at all.) Allowing parents to bring infants to work for a period of time offers a way out of this no-win predicament: relief, support, and community through the transition back to full-time work.

Sarah is one woman who found this to be true. A professor of law, Sarah did not participate in a formal babies-at-work program; she just found a way to do it. "When my son was very little he would just sleep in a sling while I worked on my computer or made photocopies or tracked down books in the library on my nonteaching day. I am lucky to have an office to myself, so it was easy to nurse or change diapers in privacy." Though she primarily brought her baby to work on her administrative day, Sarah also "wore" him while she was teaching when she didn't have to lecture for hours on end. In one session "the students watched a video of oral arguments during the class, so I introduced the film at the beginning and then paced in the back of the room with the baby in the sling during the rest of the class. I also wore him during a few informal study-skills presentations where I was moderating a panel of student speakers. This was easy to do when he was little, because I could just nurse him right before class and was guaranteed a one-hour nap while class was going on."

Virtually no crying (for baby or mom!), no separation anxiety, no temptation to find a more family-friendly work environment. Taking the baby to work allowed Sarah to remain a committed professional. Sarah was able to continue breastfeeding her infant, a practice that has been documented to reduce the infant's risk of sudden infant death syndrome (SIDS), diabetes, obesity, and asthma. It also lowers rates of certain cancers and osteoporosis in mothers. Further, increased breastfeeding rates can potentially decrease annual health care costs by $3.6 billion in the United States.[5] And healthier children mean fewer missed workdays for parents, a significant productivity bonus for employers.

Yet despite the reams of evidence and scientific recommendations that mothers feed their babies breast milk exclusively for the first six months, studies show only 12.3 percent of mothers in the United States do so.[6] Partly to blame is the need to return to work—with many women returning as early as a month to six weeks after birth, a time when many women and their babies are just finding the rhythm of their breastfeeding routine. "I see tons of women who have return-to-work dates looming and are still struggling to establish breastfeeding," says lactation consultant Jennifer Aist (who also brought each of her four babies to work with her). As a result, some mothers choose not to go back to work at all and others stop breastfeeding or choose not to start in the first place. Lower-wage workers are particularly stressed by the birth of a child in that they are less likely to have any paid leave or the resources that would enable them to take time off or take advantage of the Family and Medical Leave Act, if it is available to them. As a result, some mothers find it necessary to go back to work weeks, or even days, after giving birth. Many have no way to follow AMA recommendations to exclusively breastfeed their child for six months. Not only do they lack a *place* to pump, they almost certainly don't have sufficient break time to pump. A babies-at-work program can make all the difference for these mothers and babies.[7] Babies-at-work programs make breastfeeding feasible, and benefits accrue to baby, mother, and employer. The baby gets the best diet and the mother gets to continue in her role as excellent worker or professional.

MAKING BREASTFEEDING AT WORK EASIER

On June 11, 2009, Rep. Carolyn Maloney (D-NY) introduced the "Breastfeeding Promotion Act of 2009," federal legislation designed to promote and protect breastfeeding and pumping. To accomplish this, the bill amends Title VII of the Civil Rights Act of 1964, adding in protections for women breastfeeding in the workplace. The bill would explicitly provide that "breastfeeding and expressing breast milk in the workplace are protected conduct." The bill also seeks to establish tax credits for employer expenses incurred while promoting or supporting breastfeeding in the workplace.

Bringing a baby to work is not only an efficient and effective transition between childbirth and a return to paid employment, it can also replace anxiety with confidence. Sayre, a communications professional who returned to her job after two months of leave—far earlier than she would have dreamed of if she weren't bringing her baby to work—found herself more confident in her mothering skills because of it. "I didn't think coming into this that it would be that doable," she confesses, "but I surprised myself because I realized that I can work and be a mom at the same time and do well at both."

Babies and Coworkers: Issues to Address

Attorney Brian Moline's secretary heard him one day muttering and talking, playfully denying someone a request. But as far as she could tell, no one was in his office. Minutes passed and she realized there was, in fact, someone there: a baby. The baby's arms were outstretched from the "walker" that supporter her, as if to say "pick me up and hold me"—which Brian did regularly throughout the day.

That Brian had difficulty withstanding the beautiful girl's charms may not surprise you, until you find out that he was not her father. Instead he was the boss of the baby's mother. Not just the boss but also a skeptic of the babies-at-work program when it was implemented by his manager. After the first baby came to work, he went from naysayer to the program's biggest supporter, the "biggest sap in the world" when it came to the babies of other attorneys in the office. Brian went on to advocate for implementation of a babies-at-work program in his subsequent job as well.[8]

Like Brian, some coworkers and other members of an organization might have concerns about a babies-at-work program, fearing the babies will make too much noise or otherwise disrupt the work. But the reality of a well-structured babies-at-work program is far different from what people fear. In one study of such a program, 88.5 percent of the participants' coworkers surveyed felt the presence of the babies had no effect on their job productivity or their ability to complete tasks on time.[9] Crying— perhaps the single biggest concern of managers considering an infant-at-work program—is diminished in part because the work environment is so stimulating. With so much social interaction, visual stimulation, and access to a parent, babies are quieter and more content than anyone anticipates.

Another potential concern about a babies-at-work program is that people who are not parents or those with older kids might resent what they perceive to be special treatment for these workers. Sayre reports the opposite happened to her, saying that many coworkers told her "what a great thing" she did. "People that I would normally not interact with from other departments have been open to helping me out by taking her for ten-minute increments or just walking her around the office. Having her here has brought out really great sides of people that I would not have known about before. I never knew our middle-aged IT guy was so good with babies—but he is Audrey's number one fan here!"

Research shows that those experiences are fairly representative. Often people think right off the bat, "I don't like other people's kids" or "I'm not really a baby person," and this is reinforced by a society that has lost touch with the community's role in parenting. "What happens [with babies-at-work programs] is 'someone else's kid' becomes a person with character and a personality," says Moquin of the Parenting and the Workplace Institute. "They become 'Elise' or 'Eli' instead of 'a coworker's baby.' The community that develops becomes effortless." And as with other programs where clients and customers appreciate an employer's partnership with and respect of workers, customers also appreciate seeing the babies and get a feel for what that says about a business. In place of the expected disapproval that a workplace isn't businesslike, Alicia Lionberger of Foris Vineyards Winery, an Oregon vintner with a babies-at-work program, had the experience that customers came in simply to check on her baby's progress, even getting down on the floor to play with him—and then going home with another bottle or two of wine![10]

Having babies in the workplace is an overall morale booster. In a study of a babies-at-work program, 46.1 percent of the coworkers surveyed felt the babies somewhat or greatly increased their job satisfaction.[11] And as Brian's behavior illustrates, one of the least anticipated benefits is the instinctive community that goes into effect once the baby comes into the workplace. If "it takes a village"—a community—to raise a child, it also "takes a baby" to bring out the underlying community in many work organizations.

ON-SITE DAY CARE

Some parents prefer on-site day care to caring for a baby while at work. This is a great option when it is available; the children are close and accessible, mothers can take breaks and breast-feed infants, and most on-site care facilities keep regular business hours, so workers don't have to leave early to retrieve kids from day care or preschool. However, the start-up costs, which include finding or setting aside dedicated space within or near the company, recruiting and retaining caregivers, and handling liability insurance and regulatory issues, put this option out of reach for most businesses. Yet research done by economist Rachel Connelly shows that on-site day care might prove economically beneficial to businesses that employ blue-collar workers—parents most in need of accessible, affordable care and perhaps least able to take advantage of babies-at-work programs. Studies showed that a majority of workers were willing to pay between $125 and $225 per year to subsidize on-site day care for the company, whether or not they would use it.

As is, only 10 percent of larger companies have made the decision to provide on-site care, and only 5 percent of companies overall, providing a small pool for prospective employees looking for this benefit. Unlike babies-at-work programs, pilot programs or trial runs are not feasible, and this is clearly not an option that will work for just one or two employees who want to pitch it to their boss.

Though relatively rare, on-site care either provided by or sponsored by the employer is a saving grace to some parents. Veronica Sarossy, a development manager for the Silicon Valley games company Entertainment Arts, was one of those lucky few. EA contracts with Children's Creative Learning Center for on-site day care, and it provides subsidies of $50 per child per month for each employee. Spots are limited, but Sarossy was fortunate enough to obtain one for her son Bryce when he was four months old. Bryce just turned five and will enter kindergarten this year; overall, he has spent four and a half years—most of his young life—in on-site care. Veronica calls having Bryce on site "wonderful." In addition to loving what he's learned in his program, she does not "need to worry about school ending at noon and finding extended day care or a family member to pick him up and babysit," a plus for her employer as well.

How to Make Babies-at-Work Work for You

The key to making a babies-at-work program work is to set it up properly and carefully—sound advice for any new workplace practice. Clear communication and formal rules are critical. The Parenting in the Workplace Institute offers interested businesses template policies, like the one included at the end of this chapter, so that no one has to reinvent the wheel. "Anticipate the pitfalls and make provisions for them before they arise," Moquin advises. When the program is set up carefully and formally, and tailored along the way to each company's specific situation, parents work hard to make it a success and gain new motivation to do their work efficiently and well. When managers establish that this type of program is a privilege and not an automatic benefit, and also stipulate that the arrangement must be sustainable for everyone if it is to continue, they alleviate concerns that a pilot program may wed the company to the benefit even if it's not working.

Successful babies-at-work programs have several common denominators that have been scrupulously documented by the Parenting in the Workplace Institute:

- Determine rules of engagement.
- Set standards of eligibility.
- Remember that coworkers are not babysitters.
- Provide privacy.
- Use common sense.
- Address liability concerns—don't agonize over them.

Determine Rules of Engagement

As with any agreement between two parties (or more), spelling out concrete terms and provisions for bringing an infant to work—and having both parties sign and agree to the terms—

greatly increases the chance of success. According to the Parenting in the Workplace Institute, of the more than 120 successful babies-at-work programs it has examined, nearly every one has structured guidelines in place. Conversely, the only companies in which baby programs have not worked were ones in which there were no expectations or rules. If babies were left to cry for too long, or if guidelines weren't in place to prevent coworkers from playing with the babies too much (and thus reducing productivity), the program didn't work. One of the rules that must be agreed to is what Moquin calls the "safety valve," or the right to terminate the program for an employee. In the unlikely event a baby at work just isn't working out, having a safety valve in place offers the employer (and coworkers) a measure of security.

It's important to lay out two stipulations that operate synergistically to increase success for both the parent and the company. The first is one that all parents already feel in their gut: the baby's needs come first. If both the employee and the boss agree that parents' first responsibility is to their infants, it is likely that each baby will be cared for as needs arise, reducing the chances for meltdown crying or tantrums and more stress for the parent and everyone else involved. It is also critical that the company's operations go on and that production not be compromised—the second stipulation. Bringing a baby to work is not the same as taking parental leave; a parent who is at work is expected to fulfill whatever set business goals and job responsibilities have been drafted prior to the plan's implementation. For a baby-at-work program to succeed, participating parents and coworkers must be able to get their work done.

While employees are expected to perform their jobs and accomplish their goals, the way work gets done might change temporarily. Instead of pumping in a closet, Sayre, the communications professional, says, "It is now quite common for me to type an e-mail, edit an article, update the Web site, or sit in on a conference call while I am breastfeeding." There is an increase in parental efficiency that anyone with children will recognize. "I find that I get my work done in quick spurts now," says Sayre. "While she is sleeping, while someone is holding her, while she is occupied with a toy or while I am typing with one hand and playing with her with the other hand. Honestly, there are days where I get less done than I aim to, but I usually will do some work from home if I need to. I am also more aware of my limitations now—if I know I can't do something in a certain time frame, I will see if my coworker can handle the job instead or I just let my coworkers know."

Some employers with formal programs reduce employees' pay for this time, paying a worker for about thirty hours of a full-time schedule, assuming that about two hours spent at the office each day will be used to care for the baby. However, a reduced pay scenario is actually the exception, not the rule. Nearly all companies actually keep the parent's compensation the same, finding that the work evens out when parents stay late to finish a job, which, not haunted by a day-care pickup time, they're able to do more easily. And participating parents work more productively in the time that they have devoted to work duties. "I got really used to power working!" confessed lactation consultant and babies-at-work participant Jennifer, who even brought her infant twins to work.

Though Jennifer worked more productively, she, too, depended on help—with receptionists sometimes holding a baby. The logistics meant it was not always easy. During those months, she says, she would often wonder about the freedom of dropping the kids off at day care, though in the end it was more than worth it: "I would do it again in a heartbeat." Overall, our research showed that if employers are willing to be flexible and supportive and if guidelines are clearly spelled out and agreed to, a babies-at-work arrangement will generate benefits for years to come—a small price to pay for logistical changes spanning a few months' time.

Set Standards of Eligibility

Both full-time and part-time employees should be eligible for babies-at-work programs, as well as workers across the spectrum of responsibilities and positions. And employees whose job duties are not well-suited to the program should be able to discuss opportunities for temporary reassignment within the company that would make using the program feasible; however, the employer is not required to grant the request. Employees should be in good standing with their companies to participate in a babies-at-work program. This includes having completed any probationary period and being free of any outstanding disciplinary action related to work.

Babies need to meet eligibility requirements, too. As any parent knows, there is a big leap between a gurgling two-month-old whose big workout is "tummy time" and a mobile baby, exploring and pulling up on everything. Babies-at-work programs have the best results by limiting the time the infant spends at work to 240 days of age or until the baby learns to crawl, whichever comes first. This time frame allows the worker to bond and socialize with a newborn. It also allows time to arrange for ongoing care more appropriate to an older baby.

Even in their least active stage, not all infants will mesh with the workplace. Anyone who has spent time with a colicky baby knows they don't make good office mates. When Stu brought his slumbering infant into work for a day, and plopped the bouncy chair on a conference table, his colleague Sarah, whose own baby had suffered through months of colic, couldn't stop staring at the infant and saying, "So that's what babies can be like." Yet even if an infant goes through a fussy stage where other arrangements are necessary, the workplace can still be a good fit once the child grows out of a difficult stage. And more good news: babies that are held and fed on demand tend to be calm.

Remember That Coworkers Are Not Babysitters

Some coworkers, especially those without children, may feel uneasy about babies in the workplace because they feel they will be tapped as impromptu caregivers when the parent is unavailable. While experience shows that most coworkers actually enjoy the occasional cuddle and saying hello to the baby, success follows those that formally appoint one or two alternate care providers who volunteer in advance to stand in when the main parent is unavailable—be it for a bathroom break or a critical conference call. However, if the baby becomes fussy for long periods of time, it is up to the parent to temporarily remove the baby to a quiet room or from the workplace.

Provide Privacy

To protect privacy and respect the parent and coworkers alike, companies should choose a designated spot for feeding, if the parent desires, as well as appropriate locations for changing. Having to put up with a coworker's esoteric cubicle decorations is one thing, but breathing eau de dirty diaper is quite another!

Having a private physical space is also important for those occasions when the baby might disrupt the normal flow of business. Even still, Jennifer, the lactation consultant who brought all four of her babies to work, admits that "there was a lot of pressure to keep the baby quiet and happy." When those rough spots do emerge, it's helpful if parent and child can go behind closed doors. Sayre thinks that's a key to success. The catch in Sayre's case was that she did not have her own office—she worked in a cubicle. The solution was for her boss, the director of communications, to give Sayre her office to use for the six months the baby was there. "My boss now sits in my cubicle, with no privacy! I think she sets a great example for other supervisors here to accommodate those employees they manage."

Use Common Sense

A baby who is sick should be at home, not in a parent's office. Successful babies-at-work programs clearly spell out under what conditions a baby shouldn't come in to work. Most companies, like many day-care centers and schools, follow the specific recommendations set out by the Centers for Disease Control for determining whether or not infants are well enough to come in. A parent who works for a company that clearly demonstrates support for family-friendly policies is less likely to feel pressured to bring in a sick baby in the first place, just as workers with a high degree of control over their schedules keep themselves home when they're sick. Additionally, babies who participate in babies-at-work programs, along with their parents, get sick less often because they aren't exposed to the germ-breeding environment of day care and because they're more likely to have the immune-system booster of breast milk.

It's also important that all parties understand that babies-at-work programs are not the same as on-site day care; the parent is the primary caregiver for the child. If a parent leaves the building for whatever reason—even to grab a coffee—baby goes too, no exceptions.

Address Liability Concerns—Don't Agonize Over Them

As a manager or business owner, the thought of instituting a babies-at-work program might tempt you to rush to the legal department. You're not alone. Liability is one of the top concerns for employers considering babies-at-work programs. To address potential liability, having the employee sign a waiver releasing the company from any liability offers tremendous protection.

(We also think a jury would be hard-pressed to punish a company that in good faith did something so generous for its employees.) Not to be discounted, Moquin told us, is the self-screening process that happens. "Parents who push to participate in this type of program tend to be very attentive, very in tune with their babies, and are focused on the kid. The odds of something happening to the child are very low—99.9 percent of the time nothing will happen."

For employers who may still be nervous, liability policies specific to babies-at-work programs are available. They provide a safety net, ensuring the company is not punished financially in the rare event of an accident, while also providing money for the child in case something unthinkable does happen. If it won't create a financial hardship, asking participants to pay the premiums for the liability policy removes some of a company's financial burden and also places more responsibility on the parent. The premiums are affordable to most parent-workers, and much less expensive than six months of day care. Liability is also inherently reduced by limiting the program to babes in arms—no more than 240 days old, *and* not yet able to crawl. An infant in a carrier is far less likely to meet with an accident than a "waddler" or toddler who can crawl or walk to the power strip or pull down a coffee pot.

Whole Worker, Whole Person

As discussed in preceding chapters, there are many ways to balance work and care for a new addition to the family, including alternative scheduling that allows for shared child-care duties within the family, downshifting or off-ramping if the family budget allows, or working from home if the job and employer can accommodate virtual options. Taking infants to work is yet another way for parents to create a custom fit between their job and personal responsibilities at a particularly demanding and joyful point in the life course. When a job is suited to this custom-fit approach, everyone involved can benefit: baby, business, and parent. Babies-at-work is a program that respects employees' off-the-job responsibilities while honoring their value to the business—as well as one that treats a good worker who is also a good parent as a whole person. And don't forget the longer-term benefits companies reap from welcoming infants to the workplace: a valued worker is retained, commitment and loyalty swell, and a winning organizational culture grows.

[SAMPLE POLICY TEMPLATE]

[Company]
Infant-at-Work
Program Guidelines

Policy

It is the policy of [COMPANY] to provide a positive work environment that recognizes parents' responsibilities to their jobs and to their infants by acknowledging that, when an infant is able to stay with a parent, this benefits the family, the employer, and society. The [COMPANY] Infant-at-Work Program encourages new mothers or fathers to return to work sooner by allowing the new parents to bring their infant to work with them until the child is [180 days old / 240 days old] or begins to crawl, whichever comes first.

Eligibility

Parents—Full-time and part-time [COMPANY] employees are eligible to participate in the program, subject to the specific job responsibilities of the parent and subject to ensuring the physical safety of the infant. Employees currently involved in disciplinary action and employees who have not completed their ___-day orientation/probation period are not eligible to participate. Employees may request a temporary alternative work assignment if their current assignment is not suitable for participation in the program. [COMPANY] will attempt to accommodate such requests based on business and staffing situations at the time of the request but is not required to meet said requests.

Infants—Infants of part-time and full-time employees [up to the age of 180 days old / 240 days old / until the infant begins to crawl] are eligible for the program, subject to the provisions of these Guidelines.

Alternate Care Providers—Parent must select two other [COMPANY] employees to provide back-up care for the infant. An alternate care provider may not simultaneously participate in the program as a parent bringing his or her baby to work and as an alternate care provider for another parent's child.

Forms to Complete
The following forms *(not provided in the book)* are required for participation in the program:

- Individual Plan, which outlines the specifics of the infant's care plan (Attachment 1)
- Parent Agreement, Consent & Waiver forms (Attachment 2)
- Alternate Care Provider Agreement (Attachment 3)

The parent will submit all completed and signed forms to the human resources manager, who will then schedule the Pre-Program Meeting.

Pre-Program Meeting
Before any infant is brought into the workplace, a meeting must take place between the parent and the human resources manager. Both parties must review, discuss, and approve the proposed Individual Plan.

Requirements for Care Providers
A parent participating in this program may not leave the building (not even for a short time) without taking the infant with them.

The parent will accept complete responsibility for the safety of the infant. If the parent's duties require that they leave their primary work site, the parent will take the infant with them. An employee may not take the infant anywhere in a [COMPANY] vehicle.

The parent must provide all supplies and equipment needed to care for the infant at the work site and ensure that the area is kept in a clean and sanitary condition. Diapers must be changed

Continued

only in a designated restroom or in quiet room locations and not in work areas. When an infant accompanies a parent to work, used cloth diapers must be stored in a closed container and taken home daily. Used disposable diapers must be wrapped appropriately and discarded in an appropriate container provided by the parent and placed in an area not used by staff for office or meeting space. All other supplies utilized by the parent must be maintained in a manner that is not disruptive to the work of other employees.

Parents must have day care or other arrangements in place by the time their baby [is 180 days old / is 240 days old / begins to crawl].

There may be work circumstances that require a parent's full attention such that it may be necessary for parents to make other arrangements for child care during these periods. Parents are expected to work closely with their supervisor and coworkers to ensure that all parties involved are aware of what duties can and cannot be reassigned and parents are expected to make alternate child care arrangements when required to do so.

In order for an infant-at-work program to be most effective, all parties need to be sensitive to the needs of others. The employee must maintain acceptable work performance and ensure that the presence of the infant does not create any office disturbances. If problems arise that cannot be resolved, the employee understands that the program may be terminated for that employee.

If a baby is fussy for a prolonged period of time, causing a distraction in the workplace or preventing the parent from accomplishing required work, the parent shall remove the infant from the workplace. The parent will be charged for time away from work according to leave time provisions of [COMPANY] or may be subject to pay deductions for missed work.

[COMPANY] will identify one or more locations on the premises that employees may use, if they so choose, while breastfeeding or otherwise feeding their infants.

Infant's Location During the Program
Workstation—Each parent shall make her/his workstation suitable for the new baby and the baby shall be located primarily at that workstation during the workday. [COMPANY] will make every effort to offer a private office, if needed, but cannot guarantee this if space constraints make it infeasible.

Quiet Room—In the event that an infant becomes noticeably fussy, loud, or uncontrollable, or exhibits any behavior that causes a distraction in the workplace or prevents the parent from accomplishing work, the parent must immediately take the infant to a sitting room until the infant calms down and is quieter. If the infant does not calm down within 30 minutes while in the sitting room, the parent must remove the infant from [COMPANY] premises.

Other Employees—The infant may be in another employee's workspace for brief intervals if the arrangement is agreed upon between the parent and the other employee. Consideration must be taken to ensure that the environment is safe for the infant at all times and that other employees are not disturbed.

Illness

A sick infant should not be brought to work. If the infant becomes sick during the day, the infant must be taken home by the parent. The Centers for Disease Control (CDC) "Recommendations for Inclusion or Exclusion" of children from out-of-home child care settings are attached hereto as Attachment 4, and are hereby adopted by [COMPANY] as a means for determining whether a baby is sick. *[CDC guidelines are not included in the book. You can obtain them at http://nrc.uchsc.edu/SPINOFF/IE/IncExc .pdf.]*

Alternate Care Providers

The parent shall choose two alternate care providers who will care for the infant if the parent needs to attend a meeting, work with a customer, go to the restroom, etc. Each care provider will have previously signed an Alternate Care Provider Agreement form (Attachment 3).

If a parent is going to be unable to care for their child at work for a period of less than 1.5 hours within a 4-hour period, the parent shall notify a care provider and place the infant in the provider's care.

If the parent is going to be unable to care for their child at work for a period exceeding 1.5 hours within a 4-hour period, the parent shall make arrangements for the infant's care outside the [COMPANY] premises. A care provider in the workplace shall not be permitted to care for an infant for a period exceeding 1.5 hours.

Continued

Other Personnel Caring for Infant

[COMPANY] understands that other personnel may ask the parent for permission to care for the infant for brief periods of time. This is acceptable at the discretion of the parent as long as the productivity of other personnel is not substantially reduced. Only the designated care providers should be asked to watch the infant if the parent is unable to care for the infant for a prolonged period of time (not to exceed 1.5 hours).

Complaints

All complaints must be made directly to the parent's immediate supervisor, department manager, or the human resources manager, by such means as may be provided. All complaints will be kept anonymous to the extent that is possible. The employee, the immediate supervisor, the department manager, and the human resources manager shall have final discretion to decide what should be done to resolve the complaint. (See Termination of Eligibility below.)

Termination of Eligibility

Parents have the right to terminate their individual agreement at any time. [COMPANY] has the right to terminate an individual agreement at any time if the parent's performance declines or if organizational needs are not being met (i.e., complaints and/or disruptions to coworkers cannot be resolved). The employee must maintain acceptable work performance and ensure that the presence of the infant does not create any office disturbances.

This agreement may also be terminated if the parent becomes involved in disciplinary action, if the parent does not comply with the terms and conditions of their Individual Plan, or when complaints have been made that cannot be resolved. Eligibility may also be terminated at the sole discretion of [COMPANY] for reasons not yet known at this time. When eligibility is terminated, the infant must be removed from the workplace. Depending on the circumstances, [COMPANY] may require immediate removal or notice may be given.

Other

The [COMPANY] Infant-at-Work Program is a voluntary option for employees, subject to approval as outlined in these Guidelines, where it is compatible with job requirements.

Other affected employees may request a "baby-free" work environment. Such requests should be made through the employee's immediate supervisor and the human resources department. [COMPANY] will attempt to accommodate such requests based on business and staffing situations at the time of the request.

Participation in the [COMPANY] Infant-at-Work Program is a privilege and not a right.

[COMPANY] expressly reserves the right to refuse participation in the Program for any reason or no reason at all or to terminate participation in the program due to business conditions or for no reason at all.

[COMPANY] expressly reserves the right to change or revise this policy with or without notice.

8

A MORE PERFECT UNION

The New Face of Labor and Custom Fits

Perhaps you are thinking about how to craft a custom fit for yourself. Maybe you're set on a compressed workweek, or thinking of how working virtually just one day a week might accomplish what you need. But what if you are part of the more than 10 percent of U.S. employees that also belong to a union? You are not immune to the pressures of limited time, too-full schedules, families, and other out-of-work commitments. You, too, are looking for a custom fit between your job and your life. The difference is that for you and other union members, negotiating for custom-fit policies and practices involves another layer of communication, and you are part of a group that will be represented as a whole when the union faces management at the bargaining table. Because the very phrase "custom fit" implies a work-life scenario tailor-made just for you, when you take the individual out of the primary bargaining conversation, what does that mean? Our research shows that when unions are aware of the diverse challenges facing their workers, in tune with the needs of a membership very different from that of a quarter century ago, and sensitive to the changing American workplace, they can help add muscle to your custom-fit negotiations and help provide real and creative solutions.

For Heather, a fifty-one-year-old nurse and member of the Service Employees International Union (SEIU), this is certainly true, and she and her coworkers depend on their union to both bargain for custom-fit options and enforce policies that are on the books but may go unused because of perceived pressure from management. For Heather and her colleagues, like so many others introduced in this book, work-life issues loom large. "Since the majority of RNs are female, we not only work, but most have additional worries and responsibilities related to children and aging parents," she said, adding that while they are lucky in that many policies to help create custom fits have been on the books for years at union hospitals, unions work to not only hold on to those policies but also make improvements with each contract negotiation. In addition to pension improvements, staffing levels, and differential increases for non-day shifts, Heather's union has worked to improve child-care access and implement innovative shifts, such as working three twelve-hour shifts, or four tens like the ones discussed in Chapter Three.[1] Unlike the trade unions, construction, or trucking, teaching and nursing have long been staffed primarily by women. In turn, policies like those in place at Heather's employer were negotiated by the union with Heather and members like her in mind.

Negotiations like the ones SEIU has made on behalf of Heather and her coworkers, contracts that include or even prioritize work-life issues, are poised to become more common, in part because of a shifting union membership that is changing priorities at the bargaining table. But unions have long been involved in attempts to forge a fit between work and life, helping to bring American workplaces an eight-hour day and five-day week. Unions have been on the forefront of efforts to combat extreme working hours and make workers and workplaces more compatible—better fits for employees with many responsibilities, talents, priorities, and even limitations. Best known for working to protect members' job security and wage and benefit increases, the union voice shapes organizational cultures. In many cases, advances in union wages and work policies spill over to benefit nonunion workers in the same jobs.[2]

We devote an entire chapter to this sector of the workforce not simply because of the sheer number of unionized workers but because unions occupy a unique place in the argument for customized work arrangements. Because unionized workers do not negotiate on their own behalf directly with their employer, it's worth a look at how factoring the union representation into the equation adds another dimension to these negotiations and look at best practices. It's also necessary to look beyond union workers and their employers and speak to the efforts of the union representatives who act as the workers' agent and are a critical part of the custom-fit conversation for this segment of workers and their employers. And the conversations around that table are changing, responding to a union labor force that has shifted dramatically in the last few decades.

The Changing Face of Labor

Contrary to many people's idea of the average union member, if you are one of the over sixteen million U.S. unionized workers today, you are more apt to be a teacher, a police officer, or a government worker—the public sector employees that now make up the majority of union workers—than an operator in a manufacturing plant. In fact, private sector union membership dropped to just 7.6 percent in 2008, while nearly 37 percent of public sector employees were unionized.[3] According to a comprehensive study recently released by the Center for Economic Policy Research, the last twenty-five years have seen tremendous demographic changes in the unionized workforce. In 1983, over half of all union workers were white men, few held college degrees, and nearly a third worked in manufacturing. Only 35 percent of union members were women.

The typical union worker was like Garland, an electrician now retired after twenty-five years in industry. During his career he belonged to several different unions—the retail clerks, the glassblowers, the United Auto Workers—which strove to make sure the workplace was fair and safe. *Fair* meant that everyone had a chance for overtime and everyone was treated with respect. *Safe* meant ensuring that construction sites were not dangerous.

"My union fought with the State of California over powder power tools that use a 22-shell to fire a pin into concrete," he says. The fight resulted in a safer tool that required only one hand to work it and licensing to operate the heavy machinery. For Garland, this fight is emblematic of the changes that unions were able to introduce into his workplace. There weren't many women in the trades, he told us, and scheduling wasn't an issue that construction sites were eager to customize.[4]

In 2008, however, nearly 40 percent of union members held at least a four-year college degree, and only about one in ten unionized workers worked in manufacturing. In fact, in a dramatic reversal from a quarter-century ago, educated workers were *more* apt to be unionized than their peers. The unionized labor force is now more racially diverse and just as likely to work in the public sector as the private.[5] The median age of the typical union worker was forty-five, that is, squarely in the middle of the "sandwich generation": the cohort faced with caring for both children and aging parents.

Perhaps one of the most striking differences is that of gender balance. In 2008, women accounted for 45 percent of all union workers. If current trends continue, women will be a majority of the union workforce before 2020. Despite their numbers, women have been traditionally underrepresented in union membership, though now we are seeing a shift.[6] (See sidebar "A Change at the Top.") In all, these statistics add up to the face of labor changing from that of Garland to that of Heather, and the same challenges faced by nonunion workers: positions and organizational cultures that don't meet their needs.

Experts agree that the demographic shift is already having a profound effect on union agendas. Anna Burger, chair of the union coalition Change to Win, concurs that the sheer number of women in the labor movement has started to shake things up: "Because of women, we don't just talk about raising wages, but about creating family friendly workplaces with sick leave, child care, and family and medical leave."[7] While women may be the ones fomenting the change, we know that the effects of work-life policies go on to benefit all—benefit those trade workers like Garland whose conversations before centered on safety and security, benefit younger Millennials with an expectation of this type of flexibility as they join the workforce, and benefit union workers like J.K., a police lieutenant in a major U.S. city who has weathered a range of work-life fits in his career.

When J.K. joined the force as a patrol officer the standard schedule was a 6/2, or six days on and two days off, which "wreaked havoc on any officer with a family." Not everyone cared. According to J.K., young gung-ho officers worked on adrenaline and made their jobs their lives, and older officers didn't seem to mind because their wives were home with the kids. But J.K. did. With a working wife and what would become a family of four, he saw his only move as changing units— detective units, for example, work regular business hours—and testing for promotions. As a lieutenant he sets his own hours, and though his kids are now in college he was there for his daughter's volleyball games and to coach his son's basketball team. The new generation of line-level officers, he says, still mostly men, are making it clear to the union that family time is important to them and a priority in how they are represented.

A CHANGE AT THE TOP

The dramatic demographic shifts in the union labor force are part of the reason why, when in June of 2009 then AFL-CIO President John Sweeney announced he was backing his lieutenant, Richard Trumka, to succeed him, the news was met with little enthusiasm. Trumka's history included three terms as president of the United Mine Workers of America, a career history that some saw as very old-guard and ill-suited to the challenge of being an "agent of change when [change is] what organized labor needs."[8] The AFL-CIO is the largest labor coalition in the United States,

Continued

consisting of fifty-six unions with approximately 11 million members. Many felt that the changing labor movement needed leadership that was likewise fresh and new and reflected the considerations of union workers as a whole.

When Trumka prevailed and was elected president in September 2009, his win wasn't what the buzz was about at the water cooler. Instead, it was that two women had been elected to top union positions: Liz Shuler as secretary-treasurer and Arlene Holt Baker as reelected executive vice president. This marked the first time in history that the AFL-CIO's leadership included two women in its ranks.[9] Now that change has reached the top, some speculate that the national direction of union policy might begin to reflect contemporary priorities that match members' needs.

Vibhuti Mehra of the Labor Project for Working Families—a national nonprofit that educates and empowers unions to organize, bargain, and advocate for family-friendly workplaces—says it is clear that change must come, and that labor has not only the potential but the responsibility to transform the American workplace. Traditional mind-sets on all sides are hard to overcome, but she's seen slow and sure progress. Mehra also says that the growing body of research is helpful and compelling, and that union organizations are taking note.[10]

A Complicated Conversation

Though in countless ways unions are helping to facilitate custom-fit solutions, there are areas where unions keep some solutions out of reach. To fully understand how unions factor into the employer-employee custom-fit conversation, it's useful to look at some of the reasons why these roadblocks occur.

A union by definition negotiates for membership as a whole, and sometimes this is to the detriment of an individual or a small group with different needs. During negotiations with management, the union rightly focuses on what it understands to be its members' most critical needs. Many unions have prioritized health-care coverage in these negotiations—especially over the past ten years—as a critical priority to a majority of members. Assume you are a member of such a union, but your health insurance is covered through your spouse. You might personally prioritize options like a compressed workweek that would help you balance your work and family needs, but you alone are probably not going to be successful in changing the union's priorities. If, on the other hand, you were not in a union, you would be better equipped to present a compressed workweek plan directly to your manager and receive a favorable response.

J.K.'s experience is that his union is about ten years behind the workforce. He adds, "Though there are a couple of females in leadership it's still mostly white men. Their priorities are stuck on pay, officer safety, and ownership of work divisions between the units, keeping work with the union instead of contracting some of it out to civilians who could do the work for less money." Yet like Mehra, he's also slowly seeing the change, motivated by the officers who speak up and ask for what they need. And he credits the union with holding the force to the Family and Medical Leave Act (FMLA), accommodations for pregnant officers on the job, and substantial leave for new fathers.

Other than being stuck in the past, another stumbling block: managers may be reluctant to try out a custom-fit work policy, knowing that a trial policy, while it might not work, could turn into a negotiating point for the union in the future. Employers needing to negotiate with both union and nonunion workforces may find themselves even more cautious about trying new policies.

In one such example, we talked to a human resources manager at a company that had offered innovative scheduling options to all its employees, both salaried and hourly, in a move that boosted productivity, lowered absenteeism, and increased job satisfaction. While the salaried workers are in love with their new schedules, the hourly workers, represented by their union, have consistently turned down the offer. We don't know why the union has made this decision, but several reasons seem possible: the lure of overtime pay may override the desire for flexibility, or the traditional schedule may be entrenched in the union's thinking, or the union may be wary of the offer in view of the way some companies have used schedule flexibility as a way to take advantage of workers. One of the nation's largest private employers, a big-box retailer, was accused of implementing non-standard schedules as a way to force full-time workers into part-time work. While the retailer maintained it consulted associates regarding schedules, the mega-chain suffers one of the highest worker turnover rates in the industry and remains a target of unions, according to retail consultant Burt Flickinger.[11]

In this way, union policies intended to protect workers can at times create challenges for managers who might otherwise offer a custom fit to an individual. In part, unions have found it difficult to promote flexible scheduling options because more often than not, the employer—not the worker—has control over the schedule. Unions want to protect workers from hours reduced without their consent, erratic so-called flexibility not within their control, and the lowered income that results from both practices.

Clearly, it's a complicated conversation, and one with a great deal of nuance. All parties need to beware of traditional mind-sets that might obscure commonsense opportunities. The best way for today's workers to advocate for their needs is to make those needs clear to their union representatives. And both employers and unions will benefit from employing custom-fit work options. A solid respect for workers and their lives makes these conversations authentic and finds solutions that work for all.

How Unions Can Work for Custom Fits

Nearly 75 percent of all adults working in the U.S. labor force have little or no control over their schedules, and nearly 60 percent of hourly workers cannot choose their own starting or quitting times.[12] Unions have historically organized to meet the needs of workers like these who, standing alone, would be vulnerable, but together their collective voice is powerful. Working to expand employer understanding and commitment to the multiple responsibilities of today's workforce is a worthy challenge for the modern union.

Sometimes the union's role is to protect workers from inflexible or intolerant employers who might be unreasonable when it comes to scheduling time to take a sick child or parent to the doctor, or who might fire a worker who refuses mandatory overtime. There are many work environments where asking to leave early on Tuesdays to pick up a child would jeopardize the person's promotion, whether the job is on a shop floor or in a law office. Research suggests even high-wage employees—those sought after by Fortune 500 companies—may feel they can't ask for work-life benefits without repercussions. The Families and Work Institute found close to 40 percent of working parents thought flexible options would jeopardize their jobs. Of senior executives, those with the most perceived power in the management-employee relationship, only 15 percent of women and 20 percent of men thought they could use a flexible work option without career damage. If this is the feeling at the top, it is no wonder that so many union workers relish the protection and power of collective bargaining. It also underscores the critical nature of introducing flexibility into the conversation.

Unions can ensure that workers needing time off for medical reasons can return to the same quality job they left and, as noted, have proven excellent enforcers of the Family and Medical Leave Act, which mandates that jobs stay intact for up to twelve weeks (though without pay) for workers who meet the criteria and need time off for their own health or for caregiving responsibilities.[13] Unions can also work to negotiate part-time or reduced-time options, ensuring that part-time workers get fair pay and fair benefits.

Currently, community-labor coalitions are active in fourteen states, working to advance work-life policies including family leave insurance and paid sick days and build support for various family-friendly policies at the federal level. Some of our favorite success stories include the following:

- The American Federation of Government Employees and the Social Security Administration negotiated a contract that allows employees to take off up to twenty-four hours a year for activities like parent-teacher conferences or volunteering in schools, routine family medical appointments, or elder care.

- In an innovative solution for conflicting work and school schedules, CWA/IBEW negotiated with Verizon Inc. to increase its dependent care fund; in part, the money is used to fund the "Kids in the Workplace" program aimed at parents of school-age children. It offered care for children on school holidays, about fifteen days a year, at thirty sites. Though the program was discontinued because of liability issues, this is a great example of working together to solve a common problem—kids off from school and parents needed at work. For more inspiration on dealing head-on with liability, review Chapter Seven.

- Even something as basic as swapping shifts with another worker occasionally needs a nudge at the union bargaining table. Teamsters Local 445 worked with St. Luke's Hospital in New York to allow employees to arrange their own swaps if preapproved by their supervisors.

- Service Employees International Union Local 790 negotiated a Voluntary Time Off (VTO) Program with the San Francisco Housing Authority. In addition to regular sick leave and vacation time, employees are able to take time off in increments from 1 hour to 480 hours at a stretch—the equivalent of sixty 8-hour days—per year.

Wages are taken out of the employee's next paycheck following the start of the leave. Employees taking advantage of the VTO Program remain covered by medical, dental, and life insurance and continue to accrue sick and vacation time normally. Employees thus receive extra flexibility for time off without placing an undue burden upon their employer.[14]

Unions can bring an organized method of communication to the employee-employer discussion that may not have existed otherwise. Because union organization depends upon directly speaking to workers about their needs, a rich opportunity exists for unions to ascertain those needs. The Harvard Union of Clerical and Technical Workers (HUCTW) took full advantage of this opportunity and based recruitment around building meaningful relationships with every person in the membership. In talks with future members, information came out not only about their work lives but also about their personal lives—about late nights with newborns or a kindergartner's first day of school, and union organizers saw how many employees with children faced scheduling and financial barriers to success.

Before HUCTW's first agreement with Harvard University, it built up support with the community of union members. In doing so it used what the Labor Project for Working Families says can be key in obtaining custom fits with employers and unions: joint advisory teams made up of union members and management working together toward solutions. To this day, union members and department managers sit on committees and strategize about solutions to problems, with a focus on work-life balance issues.

Additionally, rank-and-file union members serve as elected union representatives for their particular departments within the union. So if you're one of two dozen systems analysts, for instance, you might represent that group at union meetings, letting leadership know the specific needs of your department.

These practices are advisable for any union to follow. In the case of HUCTW, they led to, among other benefits, the establishment of a need-based fellowship program to help with daycare and after-school program costs, paid parental leave for new mothers and fathers, the ability to use paid sick days to care for children, and individual work-family problem solving, with support and training for individual workers and managers. HUCTW also facilitated a commitment to ongoing formal work-family discussions co-chaired by union members and management. This strategy is not only good for union members, it gives participating managers an opportunity to communicate directly with union workers, getting a good feel for their issues and concerns before the bargaining starts. Listening directly to employees improves the employee-manager relationship, and sharing concerns in this manner also allows managers to express real issues that might be keeping them from agreeing to a request. The union, in setting up these arrangements, facilitates communication and promotes creativity in reaching agreements that are mutually beneficial. (See Chapter Nine for a discussion of this sort of team approach, which levels the playing field between managers and employees, in the context of non-union workers.)

As is evident by the result of the HUCTW's efforts, when a union decides that flexibility and other custom-fit opportunities are important benefits for members, policies can change for large groups of workers. Moreover, if agreed-upon policies are not followed, the union can intervene. In Chapter Three, we wrote about the implementation gap that opens when custom-fit policies are on the books but not used. Unions have the power to close this gap by playing the role of enforcer. A study conducted by the University of California, Berkeley, and the Labor Project for Working Families found that companies with any unionized workers are nearly twice as likely to comply with the federal Family Medical Leave Act than companies without a unionized workforce. In this way, unions can play a critical role in turning policy into reality for union and non-union workers alike.[15]

Talking the Talk: Advice for Union Reps, Managers, and Union Members

This section presents some of the best advice from those working on a day-to-day basis to incorporate work-life fit into the union-employer conversation. Though we've broken it out by intended audience, the tips and ideas should be understood by all parties for the best chance at a meaningful exchange and win-win policies like those described in this chapter.

Tips for Union Negotiators

While some unions have long paid attention to custom-fit needs, others lag behind and stick to the old ways of doing business. First and foremost, union negotiators must recognize demographic shifts in play and pay attention to the changing needs of their constituents.

Second, negotiators should make use of the resources that have emerged, resources like the nonprofit Labor Project for Working Families. These resources can help unions tend to the needs of their changing membership in positive ways, from citing scores of examples of real-life successes to the development of an online labor education and resource network called *LEARN Work Family*.

Third, negotiators can benefit from the example of the HUCTW and endorse joint advisory teams. Empower members to communicate their needs, and then give them opportunities to communicate directly with their managers on an ongoing basis.

Helping union members achieve custom-fit solutions involves looking at a work culture from each and every angle. That's why The Labor Project recommends going through the following considerations before sitting down at the bargaining table:

1. Examine the current flexible work options offered by employers and explore the potential to build on existing benefits. For example, does the employer offer flexible work arrangements to management-level employees that could be extended to members of the bargaining unit?

2. Consider the scope of the negotiation. Is flexibility negotiated for the entire bargaining unit, for specific work divisions, or for individual workers?

3. Determine if flexibility is a guaranteed worker right, or if it's discretionary. If discretionary, is the decision made by the employer alone or jointly by the worker and the employer?

4. Determine the eligibility criteria for flexible or alternative schedules.

5. Examine limits and greater worker control for making flexible work arrangements. For example, look to restrictions on the frequency of shift rotations, or the number of weekends a worker may be required to work in a month, or limits on overtime.

6. Assess the impact of flexible work arrangements on workers' compensation, benefits, and seniority. For example, do workers get premium pay for working nights, weekends, or holidays? Do part-time workers get full benefits or prorated benefits?

7. Determine what allowances should be made for hardship situations and emergencies, such as an inability to secure child care on short notice or during certain work hours.

In addition to those listed, two important considerations follow research and evidence covered in the discussion on hourly workers in Chapter Three. If you're negotiating for low-income workers, check for a guaranteed minimum of work hours per week. Also, as Professor Lambert's research illustrated, consider whether the communication of schedule changes in advance might be used as a bargaining piece.

Tips for Managers

When managers sit down with union reps, it's not always easy to find a win-win. With health care, for example, the negotiation is clearly a give-and-take—someone is going to take a hit. Custom fit, by contrast, is a mutual benefit, and so managers would be well-advised to approach it that way. To take J.K. as an example, schedules have gradually shifted for the police force in his city from six days on/two days off to four days on/three days off, a change that makes an enormous difference in the lives of the officers. Another example of the mutual benefit is UNITE HERE Local 2, which offers a pioneering benefit for the hospitality workers it represents in the form of a child- and elder-care fund that provides up to $150 a month to take care of basic needs for workers' relatives. The hotels that employ the hospitality workers contribute 15 cents for every hour worked by an eligible union member. According to the fund manager Louise K. Rush, the arrangement has been a win-win. While the value to the union members may be clear, she says that management has found the benefit helps attract and retain workers, especially in hard-to-fill slots.[16]

If the UNITE HERE Local 2 program seems out of reach, start small. Managers should take a look at flexible policies already in existence. Could they be extended to other areas of the company? What might that look like? Will the needs of the union workforce be met by the policy? Does it mesh with their job duties and priorities? Third, managers should recognize that even if they don't deal with unions directly, some unions are driving creative, interesting solutions to the problem of work-life fit. Paying attention to their proposals and arrangements can give you ideas that will benefit your workers and your business.

Tips for Union Members

Some unions, such as Heather's, are already committed to including family-friendly, flexible, and innovative custom-fit policies in their negotiations with employers. Others have not yet had these priorities hit their radar, but it is only a matter of time before they do. How much time depends on the union members.

Members would be well-served to use their union strategically. Make sure you're heard. Make sure the issues that are important to you are talked about. Women especially, who have long been underrepresented in union leadership, need to be a voice and look for ways to influence negotiations. Jessica, a union journeyman electrician and new mother, does not currently have paid leave or any child-care options in her contract, but she feels free to voice her concerns. "Members are really encouraged to speak out at meetings and talk about what's important. I feel that if I were to raise the issue, I would be heard."

The Win-Win

More than just offering companies that have union members and the members themselves more opportunities to find mutual benefit, introducing custom-fit solutions also offers a chance for deeper trust, empathy, and an expansion of the union-employer conversation. Building on a long history of advocating for respect and dignity for all workers, union leadership and members can play a pivotal role moving forward by helping build the custom-fit workplace.

9

FROM HIGH STRESS TO HIGH COMMITMENT

Workplaces Rooted in Respect

Imagine doing your job well and when and how you think is best. Because you achieve your targets, no one gives you sidelong glances as you leave work early for softball, or mutters *"It must be nice"* when you come in after taking your son to school. Imagine a workplace where your manager genuinely believes the most important asset the company has is *you*, and trusts you to deliver stellar performance without hovering over your shoulder or checking when you come back from lunch. Imagine a company that puts you, the one on the production line, in charge of selecting coworkers who match your values and fit with your team. Imagine a culture of company-provided training and education where, as the target of rich investment, you help grow the company from a position of knowledge and responsibility. Does this sound too good to be true? Does this sound like a place where you'd like to work?

If you answer yes, you certainly are not alone. And that's not terribly surprising given what these workplaces have in common: a high level of mutual trust and respect between workers and employers and a shared responsibility for profitability and productivity. Though this concept goes by various names in organizational development circles, and the applications look different depending on whether workers make doors or sell software, they all fit into the broad category of "high-commitment" workplaces. This term was coined and used as far back as the 1970s by companies like General Mills and Procter & Gamble, which sought to fundamentally change their management model.[1] This shift and how it has developed is described well by Harvard Business School professor Richard E. Walton as a move from "a model that assumes low employee commitment and that is designed to produce reliable if not outstanding performance" to one where "market success depends on a superior level of performance, a level that, in turn, requires a deep commitment, not merely the obedience—if you could obtain it—of workers." He notes that "as painful experience shows, this commitment cannot flourish in a workplace dominated by a familiar model of control."[2] This chapter is all about what happens when a model of control is replaced by a model of trust.

The culture shift to high commitment, and its connection to flexible workplace practices in more recent times, was made recently by Michael Peel, now vice president for human resources and administration at Yale University. Peel was chief human resources officer at General Mills for more than seventeen years. Interviewed to discuss a Yale University employee survey published in 2009, Peel said he was delighted it showed a high degree of worker satisfaction and commitment among Yale's nine thousand employees—from clerical workers to management—with 80 percent calling Yale a great place to work.[3] In connecting both his current and former successful workplace environments—General Mills was consistently recognized by *Fortune* and *Working Mother* in their 100 Best Places to Work lists during his tenure—Peel says that great workplaces have three things in common. First, the organization needs to have a strong culture, with a mission and values shared by managers and workers. Additionally, jobs need to be challenging and managers need to be challenged to bring out the best in their employees. His final requirement, in addition to competitive compensation, is that "the organization respond[s] well to the needs of employees, particularly with the flexibility required to integrate their extremely demanding professional and personal lives."

As Peel's tripartite definition makes clear, finding a custom fit between life and work goes beyond making job sharing possible or allowing employees to work from home on Fridays. Because for employers even to offer in good faith the policies we discuss in this book, and to have employees utilize them without stigma, the practices must be grounded in reciprocal respect and responsibility. This means companies feel committed to their workers and treat them as whole people with great potential. In return, research and surveys like the one done at Yale show that workers not only go above and beyond for employers that respect their out-of-work commitments, they also commit for the long term and give their best performance. For some companies, like those in manufacturing, where shifts are more regimented and workers are required to be on-site, a high-commitment culture and employee participation, trust, and development are enough to significantly reduce turnover and absenteeism while boosting productivity.

Both large corporations and small family businesses have benefited from abandoning traditional management practices and embracing high-commitment workplace practices. Studies show that these organizations are quantifiably more productive and have turnover rates well below average. Beaulieu, a carpet manufacturer that implemented high-commitment practices, reported an increase of 20 percent in profitability for 2008, a year in which home building–related companies were taking huge hits. As a textile company, it battled persistent turnover in excess of 40 percent. Beaulieu's owner, Carl Bouckaert, had the vision to see that a change was needed. After implementing a high-commitment culture, turnover dropped by 50 percent in ten months, with estimated savings to the company of $4.2 million.[4] Gap Outlet's production and technical services teams piloted high-commitment policies that caused production turnover to drop by 50 percent, and employee engagement scores to improve by 13 percent. These workplaces decrease voluntary turnover because employees respond well to the latitude and trust.

High-commitment workplaces are not, however, havens for slackers; on the contrary, they can *increase* involuntary turnover rates when first implemented by revealing more clearly those workers who do not meet expectations.[5] Developing leadership in employees and insisting on good two-way communication reduces blame shifting and avoidance and broadens commitment to problem solving and finding solutions. These workplaces show drops in lost-time accidents and absenteeism and even lower employee theft.[6] It turns out that when all employees are expected to act in the company's best interest, and in the best interest of their coworkers, the vast majority of them do, and then some.

So if these practices are so effective, so easy to endorse as the morally correct way to treat others, and so well-studied by business scholars—for decades in some cases—why aren't they more widespread? In short: for most businesses this is scary stuff. An organizational philosophy built on trust and respect can elicit resistance from managers because of the degree of change required. It requires teams of workers to be partially self-managing and accountable. It therefore has the real potential to reduce management layers, and thus the perceived power, of those in charge. It is a bottom-up philosophy, not the traditional top-down industrial work model that most of us are familiar with. And it is not necessarily easy to make this leap. Sue Bingham, principal of HPWP Consulting, has worked with manufacturers to create high-commitment workplaces for eighteen years. She says, "People in our workshops constantly ask us, 'Why isn't everyone doing this?' The answer is because it takes courage. You can't do it without caring and courageous leaders who say 'I want to be the vendor of choice *and* the employer of choice.' It may not be the guy at the head of the company. It could be a middle manager who brings it in and changes her sphere of influence but it has to be a philosophy that fits with their values."[7]

In this chapter we ask you to take a bit of a philosophical leap. We explore adaptations of high-commitment workplaces in which "custom fit" is achieved through two different approaches to human resources management that share this vision of success. These are companies and organizations where the workplace culture we describe at the opening of this chapter is a reality, and is generating both human and business results.

The first approach is that used by HPWP Consulting in its work with large manufacturers. Though "high-performance workplace"—referred to as "HPWP"—is a term used in slightly different ways by the various consultants and organizational specialists who are experts in this particular type of practice, we will use the term as defined by HPWP Consulting: when you have a workforce that incorporates high commitment and high trust you get higher productivity in every metric—the ultimate win-win. Used to great effect, it puts ownership of work squarely on the shoulders of those who need to get it done. It encourages employees to buy in to a company wholeheartedly by giving them control over important decisions. A high-performance workplace paves the way for conversations about custom fit, because workers are empowered to voice what's working and what's not. This empowers them to work toward solutions.

The second approach is known as results-only work environment (ROWE). Based on a values system that cedes control over how, when, and where people work and expects excellent productivity and commitment from employees in return, ROWE's purpose is just that: to evaluate and manage workers based only on their results. A key component of ROWE lies in eliminating from the workplace what its creators call "SLUDGE," a term they've trademarked to describe those judgments we've all experienced about our *perceived* output, all based on a very unreliable and unproductive metric: when we're seen sitting at our desks.

HPWP and ROWE are two high-commitment possibilities out of many, but they are especially persuasive and inspiring examples of the type of culture shift that can redefine the fundamental relationship between life and work.

High-Performance Workplaces: Where People Are People

Tony is a phenomenal worker with years of experience—conscientious, dedicated, good at what he does. Though the work is challenging, he's proud of what he produces and wants to feel more invested in the company because of it. Yet something is holding him back from totally committing and giving the company his all. He feels hamstrung by policies that seem to expect the worst from him, even after years of service. He has to account for his every movement. His supervisor manages *his* employees too and micromanages him, instead of allowing him to do his work and help solve problems. New hires aren't good fits, and they just make his job more difficult—while they're there, anyway. In fact, top management's disregard for high turnover sends the clear message to Tony about his worth. Sure, Ed over in accounting *is* a slacker and hates his job; everyone knows that, but Tony and the rest of the team do great work. Tony's not Ed, so why is he treated like Ed?

He's treated like Ed because his company has lost sight of what we all know intuitively, and what HPWP Consulting avows: 95 percent of all employees are responsible and ethical and want to be great at what they do, leaving 5 percent that lack the necessary positive motivation. These aren't simply people who are falling short of top performance; any one person could experience poor job fit, need better training, or be experiencing outside problems. It's up to a good manager to help evaluate poor performance and help employees find ways to succeed. No, we're talking about the 5 percent who don't have good motives: the bad apples like Ed who aim to do as little as possible and get away with as much as possible.

While traditional management structures have people managing to the bad apple because the cost risk is measurable, the calculation is not being made of the cost of making 95 percent of the workforce abide by the policies set up to catch the 5 percent.

The risk to that management style, according to Annie Snow-barger of HPWP Consulting, is substantial, especially in the manufacturing sector. "The employees we work with are deacons in their churches, parents, PTA members, and community leaders. When we bring them into the workplace, too often we strip them of all of those positive attributes. It's demoralizing to become just a subordinate when you walk in the door." Furthermore, while most employees want to do the right thing, so do most managers. Oftentimes supervisors use outdated, traditional models because of their own lack of training and education, not knowing or believing there is a viable alternative. Even if managers are caring people, when they come to work they have to set their own values and judgments aside and enforce the existing rules consistently, even when it doesn't make sense. Both employees and managers are being robbed of their intuitive ability to solve problems and work as a team to be effective and productive.[8]

HPWP is a complete reversal, geared around supporting the vast majority of good employees through employee development and including employees in company goals and practices, making the optimization of the employee and the organization one and the same.[9] "Trust changes everything," says Jason Marion, HR director at high-performance employer Southeastern Mills. "It affects our assumptions about our employees, it allows us to make decisions faster, it makes us more profitable. Once you've created a culture of trust, everything else falls into place."

Generally speaking, high performance is a philosophy more than a specific practice, though high-performance workplaces commonly touch on the following criteria:

- Strong employee motivation and commitment is the norm.
- Employee development includes the participation and ideas of all workers.
- All workers have equal standing and treatment.
- Positions and roles are designed for performance, not by bureaucracy, and workers are cross-trained.

- Jobs are well-designed and roles fit together well.
- A strong mission and values are shared by the entire organization.
- Employees participate in team development and hiring.

Workers who feel vulnerable—whether they believe their job is on the line or they simply don't feel valued—will not work on their own behalf to find a custom fit, too afraid of reprisals. Not so in a high-performance environment where the collaborative, team approach keeps at bay the fears inherent in a hierarchical structure. If you work for an HPWP and you need to reduce your hours because your mother is sick, you don't shuffle into the boss's office, make your case, and wait for the verdict to be handed down from on high. Rather, you meet with your team and approach the problem as a group. You work in a solution-based environment, a setup designed to get to yes more quickly than anything else.

What is striking about the high-performance philosophy is that it has a proven track record for companies often overlooked in business press profiles of innovative workplace strategies. This is why the HPWP Consulting group caught our eye. Their work focuses on helping manufacturers implement high-performance systems and enabling a culture shift in a business sector often characterized by poorly treated workers and deeply entrenched divisions between workers and management. Often these businesses are the very same ones that interact with a unionized workforce, the union adding leverage to the workers' position and giving them respect and pull in terms of bargaining power. In fact, as a human resources professional just out of school and responsible for collective bargaining with unions, Ken Bingham was tasked by his employer, the construction giant Ceco, to survey successful companies with progressive management attitudes in order to learn their secrets. Those attitudes and practices became the basis of HPWP Consulting, the business he co-founded, and HPWP has helped dozens of businesses—Southeastern Mills and Beaulieu of America among them—develop high-performing workplaces with rich cultures of respect.

Southeastern Mills: Values, Vision, and Volition

Southeastern Mills, a Georgia-based company that makes breading, baking mixes, and other food for restaurants and manufacturers, boasts that it has been an HPWP company for over a decade. A large employer in a small town, the third-generation owners have continued a tradition of demonstrable commitment to the town, supporting schools, parks, and charities. They wanted to extend that support and commitment to their employees in the workplace, but didn't quite know how. This attitude meant that the company was starting off ahead of the game. Because the values, vision, and volition were already in place with the company leaders, Southeastern Mills had already accomplished the most difficult part of embarking down the high-performance road: believing that no one employee was more important than another, and seeing workers as vital parts of both the community and the company.

While some of the changes the company made may seem small—time clocks were eradicated, reserved parking went away, every employee received an e-mail address for communication and a key that opens every door in the facility—these are the building blocks of a new work culture, one so fundamentally different that the change isn't just tough for managers, it's also tough for workers—who feel like it's just a little too good to be true. "HPWP was very hard for me at first," says Eddie Turner, an operator at Southeastern Mills. "I didn't feel it was real. I bucked the system a lot because I felt like they were pretending. Now, I wouldn't trade it for anything. In other companies, you're trading hours for dollars. Here, I'm part of the team and making a difference."

The team culture is critical in a high-performance workplace. At Southeastern Mills, teamwork is now fostered through team, rather than individual, recognition; employees hold regular team meetings and address their own performance issues internal to those teams; and employees self-manage, setting their own team schedules, covering for coworkers' vacations and casual absences, rotating through jobs, and training their peers.

One of their most successful practices is the use of interdepartmental hiring teams. Such a hiring process may be familiar to many, but it's a rare practice in manufacturing spheres, where supervisors often just look at workers as "sets of hands." At a high-performance workplace, however, "their hands are important, but their minds are critical to the success of our business," says Chesley Heck, the senior director of manufacturing at Southeastern Mills.

The teams consist of five to six of the company's best performers from different departments or manufacturing areas. So Ellen from tech support may be on the team, and so is Ron from quality control. All team members' opinions, thoughts, and conclusions are given equal weight and consideration with no deference to rank. The team decides whether a candidate will receive an offer, and decisions are reached through consensus. Consensus means every team member must agree to live with the team's decision, whether that decision is to extend an offer or not. Southeastern Mills has a waiting list of qualified applicants and an average turnover rate of 4 percent in an industry where the average is nearly five times that. Building trust and accountability into such a critical and fundamental process as hiring has produced an incredible result, including increases in efficiency often exceeding 100 percent, occasionally 150 percent.[10]

While some managers may feel uncomfortable giving up control over such an important and costly decision as new hires, consider the benefits of equalizing the responsibility. According to Sue Bingham, the by-products include people preferring to work short-handed rather than hire a bad employee. For those they do hire, the team becomes invested in helping them succeed, taking responsibility and ownership of the decision. As a result, teams take any turnover (voluntary or involuntary) as their problem—and the reduction in turnover is almost immediate.

For Southeastern Mills, not only do high-performance values guide how managers interact with employees, they also guide interactions with consumers, a promise of integrity that doesn't go unnoticed. President Linda Owens credits HPWP with enabling the company "to build a team dedicated to customer service and continuous improvement. HPWP breeds a culture of service with employees who will do anything for our customers. This has given our company a real business advantage." That is what we call a win-win.

Beaulieu: Weathering Hard Times Together

In addition to reducing turnover and absenteeism and increasing productivity, high-performance workplaces are resilient, able to withstand market lows and stay competitive, as Beaulieu of America demonstrates. The largest carpet-only producer in the world, U.S.-based Beaulieu employs six thousand people and operates more than thirty facilities, but size alone does not make a company immune to hard times. In 2008, the economy—and new construction rates along with it—took a precipitous dive. As the carpet industry fell by 30 percent, manufacturers all began closing plants, save one.

Beaulieu had already implemented high-performance practices like hiring teams, and solution-based problem solving had replaced progressive disciplinary action. The first year the company saw turnover cut in half with estimated savings of $11 million. But with the industry in a tailspin, it wasn't enough. Instead, in late 2008 Beaulieu instituted "Rolling Right Sizes," a program in which every employee, from the company president to the line operators, took one week off without pay every ten weeks. The Rolling Right Sizes concept came from Beaulieu's tailoring and expansion of the high-performance practices. Beaulieu kept paying employees' benefits and helped workers apply for unemployment for the weeks without pay. In early 2009, another Rolling Right Size was needed. According to President Ralph Boe, the company was only able to take this action instead of more drastic measures "because we have this tremendous foundation of mutual trust and respect. We wouldn't have been nearly as successful without it."

The company as a whole agreed to make it through hard times, and the company as a whole was able to jump back to work when business picked up in the spring of 2009. It even increased market share because some competitors closed. Overall, by not laying off employees and closing plants, and by spreading the privation through the company as a whole, the Rolling Right Sizes actually had a very positive impact on employees. In addition to keeping their jobs and their benefits at a time when unemployment was rising, in the words of one worker, "I feel like they've got my back." Beaulieu was able to demonstrate its commitment and loyalty to its employees while immediately cutting costs by 10 percent, and workers felt their trust level increase substantially, and were even moved to write letters to the local papers praising their employer. When was the last time you wrote a letter to the editor praising your employer?

How does a company begin down the road toward a high performance workplace? First, roll up your sleeves; high-performance isn't about talk, it's about action, and it takes time to rewire behavior patterns. "If you're operating as a traditional manager, then you've trained your employees to be traditional responders," says Del Land, Beaulieu's CFO. "Don't get your feelings hurt when you hang a poster on the wall that says 'We Trust Employees' and they don't respond. You have to *behave* differently." It all starts with assuming the best:

- *Adopt a management vision to recognize people as people.* In a high-performance work environment, employees are whole people with skills and lives; they are not just subordinates.
- *Manage to the 95 percent.* Design workplace practices that expect the best of workers. Those who don't wish to do

their best will reveal themselves without tailoring management to out them.

- *Identify and eliminate signifiers of second-class citizenship.* Executive dining rooms, reserved parking, and resources distributed based on seniority instead of need all signal to employees they lack value and significance.
- *Implement interdepartmental hiring teams.* Distribute responsibility and tap into the experiential knowledge that workers already possess.

High-performance workplaces infuse the work culture with a team approach and respect. In thinking of the company as a more lateral team, high-performance workplaces lay the groundwork for long-term growth and success and the full respect and development of each and every team member.

Results-Only Work Environments: Getting It Done

Also dependent upon respect, the results-only work environment (ROWE) rejects the philosophy that presumes workers are "like children who, if left unattended, will steal candy."[11] In 2003, two managers at Best Buy—Cali Ressler and Jody Thompson—found their top performers awash with untenable stress levels and unrelenting on-site demands at the same time the company was launching a major campaign. They wanted to reduce this workplace stress and work-life conflict and to spur creativity and innovation, all while maximizing productivity and growth. What if, they wondered, workers were empowered to create their own goals, and then charged with reaching them without constant oversight? Ressler and Thompson went to their managers with the proposal for a ROWE, and their managers agreed to try it out.

A stealth ROWE campaign began in the form of a pilot program, enlisting 320 people to try out different flexible options, including reduced hours, virtual work, compressed workweeks, and traditional flextime. Word soon spread up the management chain. Opposition came from all sides and echoed fears that flexibility elicits from many: managers would no longer be in control, in-person collaboration would disappear, and an erasure of the line between work and personal time would mean work would never end. Slacking employees would dump their work on more conscientious colleagues. Where was the fairness? Older workers had sacrificed personal time for their careers; younger employees should have to do so as well.[12] And could it last? Would stigma attached to those who used the options gradually cause attrition? Did the options provide enough flexibility to address employees' most pressing challenges?[13]

Though some opposition continues, time and results have gradually changed minds. Today, nearly 80 percent of Best Buy's corporate headquarters is a ROWE. Employees are healthier, happier, more productive, more engaged, and more communicative. Managers have well-defined jobs they like and better relationships with staff. The company attracts better talent and enjoys a free public relations boost for trying out a workplace philosophy based on trust.[14]

So what is a ROWE, exactly? In broad terms, it focuses managerial attention on output (was the product high-quality? delivered on time? did the worker hit the promised numbers?) while disregarding traditional productivity metrics (number of absences or hours worked). *BusinessWeek* described it in futuristic terms: a "post-face time, location-agnostic way of working."[15] In practice, several tenets supply its foundation, and are critical for any organization wanting to be a ROWE:

- *ROWE requires measurable goals.* These goals may take the form of the number of hours that need to be billed per year, or the amount of money an employee is expected to bring in, or the delivery of a product to a client. The focus of workers and management alike is on the work completed, period.

- *Employees do not need management approval to participate in flexible workplace options.* If Karen is training for a marathon and wants to do her long runs in the mornings, she doesn't need to ask her manager if she can come in at 10. As long as she gets her work done, she can come in whenever she pleases. Karen and her manager, Rashida, sat down together at the beginning of the year and determined Karen's goals; as a result, Rashida doesn't need to worry about Karen's schedule and is freed up to focus on her own objectives.

- *There are no individual guidelines for flexibility arrangements.* Karen can mix and match flex options as she sees fit. She can come in to the office for an hour or two after her morning run, leave at 2 PM to work from the library for several hours, go home and work the whole night, and take the next day completely off. Not only can Karen do this, but so can Bill in an entirely different department. Their choices are not dependent upon the permission of their respective managers or the reasons they have for needing or wanting flexibility.

- *Communication technology is intrinsic.* ROWE couldn't have existed twenty years ago. Workers really couldn't do their jobs unless they were in the office, without slowing down the pace of business and threatening the bottom line. Not true today, when Karen can log onto the company server at 10 PM, e-mail a report the next morning at 6, and videoconference with Rashida to discuss it at 9. ROWE reasons that technology has given us this ability, so why treat workers like they're producing widgets from nine to five? It's clear that most aren't and don't need those parameters. You don't necessarily need to be in the office; you just need to get the work done.

Control and accountability rest with the employees, as opposed to a traditional model where supervisors are often forced into a paternalistic role (and employees into that of the child). But it takes some work to set up an effective system of accountability, work that represents both ROWE's greatest challenge and its greatest promise. With many jobs, the challenge is that people are given a title, and even a thorough job description, but if you were to ask them what they do for a living, what correlation would their day-to-day tasks have with the goals and objectives of the job? An employee may go to work each day secure in the knowledge of being an assistant regional manager, and put in the time doing assistant regional manager-type tasks. It's not necessarily clear what the job's measurable goals and tasks are. What *is* clear is that the employee will get dinged for taking a longer-than-usual lunch break.

ROWE operates in the opposite way. ROWE clarifies the work, it clarifies that assistant regional manager's goal, and as a result, it serves as a source of motivation. Workers like having clear communication about what's expected of them. It's true that clarifying and formalizing goals requires a lot of work on the front end, for the manager and for the employee. But ROWE or not, every business benefits from clear purpose and objectives.[16]

Guidelines for Making ROWE Stick

Gap Outlet had a problem. The company was watching women it had carefully trained and developed walk out the door to jobs that provided them better balance for their families and their lives. The company had already tried implementing no-meeting Friday afternoons. It had held classes on conducting meetings effectively, to cut down on wasted time. It had even given laptops out to employees to support virtual work. But it hadn't found the formula for custom work-life fit needed to retain a 76 percent female workforce in one of the most expensive and worst commute cities in the country. Its management recognized the problem and was invested in keeping these workers, but informal, ad hoc flexibility wasn't enough. Something more was needed.[17]

Inspired by Best Buy's success with ROWE, in February 2008, Human Resources Vice President Eric Severson launched a

ROWE pilot program for Gap Outlet's technical services and production teams. Finally, success: turnover in the production team was cut in half and employee engagement scores improved to become the best in the division. Building on the results, the pilot was expanded six months later to include seventy-nine additional employees. And participants see the program as a huge asset, one that makes Gap Outlet an employer of choice. As one pilot participant said, "I was recruited very strongly for another position outside the company with slightly better pay but much closer to my home. I can honestly say that if it wasn't for [ROWE], I would have taken that job."[18] In part, Gap Outlet's initial success can be attributed to the careful preparation—a three-step process—that human resources employed to prepare for the shift to ROWE. It's a process any company considering launching a ROWE would do well to consider:

- *It begins with training.* Before implementing the pilot program, participants were taught the philosophy of ROWE and became well-versed in its tenets listed earlier in this chapter, under "Results-Only Work Environments." As with high-performance workplaces, introducing ROWE requires a dramatic culture shift in order to work.
- *Manage the change.* Gap Outlet supported the pilot with ongoing communication. Both a ROWE participant Web page and a ROWE e-mail box were established. In addition, a change agent team was created, consisting of leaders from each of the pilot teams.
- *Measure the results.* One of the most persuasive tools in overhauling management structures is good data. GAP Outlet measured results by surveying both stakeholders and employees before and after the pilot project.[19]

Like all business models that depend on and trust in the best actions of employees, ROWE is a change that elicits measurable results by optimizing employees' ability to engineer their own custom fit, and by providing clear, measurable goals for achievement. Though management buy-in is key, and as with other programs, having believers who champion a practice's efficacy persuades disbelievers, the single most important insight of ROWE is this: workers will go to bat for their employers when work becomes about the work—and not about face time, office politics, or the pecking order.

Girl Scouts Go ROWE

When you hear the word "radical," Girl Scouts don't immediately spring to mind. Yet the Girl Scouts of America of San Gorgonio County, California, is one of the pioneering organizations to embrace the ROWE philosophy.

The new CEO of the San Gorgonio Girl Scouts reported she was struggling with reconciling a hundred years of nonprofit organization traditions and "we've always done it that way" attitudes with more modern ways of managing when she took the job. Despite implementing basic flexible policies, things just weren't changing as much as they needed to—in lowering stress or inspiring a fertile creative spirit. This was when the CEO spied and read Ressler and Thompson's book on ROWE implementation, *Why Work Sucks and How to Fix It*. Its message was a revelation. In less than a month, a ROWE program was rolled out to all eighty employees, complete with ROWE T-shirts and an explanatory PowerPoint that communicated the gist: (only) results matter.

In the Girl Scouts organization, employees were asked to write their own "results" by which their work performance would be judged, then review them with a supervisor. The HR director had final authority for approval. Similarly, staff were surveyed about how they wanted to handle leave time policies; they overwhelmingly chose a hybrid model in which vacation and personal time was unlimited, given the employees were on track, combined with an extended leave accrued sick time policy that kicked in after a staff member was out for three days.[20]

ROWE produced both quantitative and qualitative improvements for the Girl Scouts. While retailers look for rising profits and to keep paying customers happy, this nonprofit serves fifteen thousand diminutive cookie saleswomen and five thousand volunteers in Southern California. Anecdotal evidence pointed to ROWE contributing to better relationships and communication between staff and volunteers. Voluntary turnover also decreased, offering the organization meaningful cost savings. Staff surveys pointed to other measurable results, like a 400 percent increase in the number of employees who reported feeling "good" or "great" about their work-life balance post-ROWE, including 88 percent who affirmed that "ROWE allows me to spend more time with my family." Perhaps more unexpected, workers became healthier, with the number of employees who lost three or more hours of work time per month due to illness decreasing by 82 percent. Maybe the most significant statistic is one that underscores how treating workers as adults and giving them more control at work results in the near universal (93 percent) employee verdict, "ROWE has made me feel more in control of my life."[21]

The New Management Model

Corporate retailers, manufacturers, and even nonprofit organizations are breaking free of old ideas about how people should work and managers should manage. Their operating philosophies ask for and earn respect and commitment instead of depending on stress and control, and as a result their workplaces see improved business and personal results. High-commitment organizations—and other organizations innovating with flexible work, virtual work, babies-at-work, contract work, and redesigned jobs—are examples of how companies, leaders, and employees are reinventing how, when, and where we work. They recognize that eliciting loyalty is great business—and forcing loyalty, impossible. Helping people find a custom fit among their work and life responsibilities, recognizing that a worker is a whole person, and reaping the tangible and substantial business rewards—this is the recipe for success in building the twenty-first-century workplace.

10

THE CUSTOM-FIT FUTURE

Moving Forward

A changing of the guard is under way. New managers are replacing old, leaders are becoming more comfortable with new ways of working—flexibly, virtually, results-focused, fast- or slow-lane, with a baby strapped in, off-site and out-of-sight. But will the change happen fast enough to meet the needs of today's workforce and keep businesses and the country competitive? Many companies have at least begun to explore creative, custom work arrangements. But many others have not. Why? No matter how good the idea, initiating and implementing change in an organization is hard. At a gut level, familiarity feels safe. Change requires new mind-sets.

Even when we can see that the custom-fit workplace works, we are still quick to think it's too good to be true, that surely we've been getting away with something and are about to get caught. Take the example of SAS Institute, named by *Fortune* magazine in 2010 as the best company to work for in the United States.[1] From this North Carolina software company's inception, founder Jim Goodnight did not want employees to have vacant lives outside work. The standard workweek is thirty-five hours, employees have control over their work schedules, and they have an enviable menu of benefits to create a work-life fit, such as three to four weeks of vacation, unlimited sick days to care for themselves or a family member, health and fitness centers, and "learning centers" for child care.

Goodnight says that his employees are his greatest asset; the perks provided at SAS are an investment. Indeed, SAS has been extraordinarily profitable for more than thirty years: in 2009, its revenues exceeded $2.3 billion, up 2.2 percent from 2008.[2] All this was good news, and yet when Steve Lohr of the *New York Times* wrote, in November 2009, about competitors like IBM entering SAS's market, he concluded that the SAS way of business must be "under threat as never before," and predicted belt-tightening for what one analyst called the "big, fatted cow."

SAS is still seen as the rule-breaker about to get caught, a mind-set that persists despite its decades of longevity and stellar performance. Those of this mind think the way to compete more successfully is to move backward, toward work models of yesterday. The SAS magic *is* its respectful, flexible, employee-friendly workplace practices that engender trust and create a culture of loyal, high-performing workers. We'd be more worried for SAS if its competitors had plans to adopt SAS's culture and workplace practices rather than just its product line.

The SAS example underscores the challenge of changing mind-sets. How long will it take before people can adopt new ways of working without looking over one shoulder to see who might catch them in the act? Possibly not that long. If it's true that people have to get uncomfortable before they're willing to stick their necks out, it's also true that that time has come—we *are* uncomfortable. Consider:

- In a 2009 survey, 55 percent of Americans—across age and income levels—said they are not satisfied with their jobs.[3]
- Dual-earning couples are working more hours than ever: on average they work ninety-one hours per week combined—an increase of ten hours since 1977.[4]
- Over half of senior executives see their companies as less innovative than the competition. The biggest reason: lack of appropriate personnel.[5]

- Thirty percent of workers want to reduce their commuting costs and time.[6]
- Workers of all ages and ranks—even executives in Fortune 500 companies—say they want more flexibility and will forgo pay for it.[7]

These numbers show the problem. They suggest that we are reaching the tipping point—that it's time for meaningful change.

A Call to Action

The phrase "custom fit" reminds us that there is no one-size-fits-all answer to the problem of managing work and life. For high-tech companies, the solution may be a combination of results-only management and virtual work. Cisco, for example, gives all employees the core technology they need to be productive anyplace, anytime—thereby freeing them to just get the work done. For schools, the best solution for teachers who are parents of young children may be job sharing. For professional service firms and organizations of knowledge workers, the solution for many may be several career lane changes. For some hourly workers, taking an infant to work may keep them from losing income that could send them over the edge.

Companies like SAS, Johnson Moving and Storage, 1-800 Contacts and others profiled in this book are inspiring examples of what is possible in the realm of custom fit. But all of us have a role in moving toward a future where the custom-fit workplace is the norm. Here is what we can do:

- *Managers:* Take the lead.
- *Executives:* Champion new ways to work.
- *Human resources professionals:* Spur the dialogue.
- *Public policy makers:* Speed the change.

Managers: Take the Lead

Managers are on the front line of work-life conflict when it arises for an employee. Often this means accommodating workers who need custom work arrangements in a one-off way. Necessity is often the first reason a person seeks out a custom fit. An employee with a broken leg may only be able to work from home, virtually. A new mother may have no choice but to ask to bring her baby to work. Employees ask to swap shifts, so one can take a parent to the doctor and another can attend a school play. In this way, employees may help their managers see the value of creating custom work arrangements.

This change out of necessity can transform into a more programmatic approach. Managers can credibly make the case to upper management for customized and flexible work solutions. A key here is to focus on the business case and strategic imperative of custom fits to increase loyalty, retain talent, spur innovation, promote a culture of satisfied and engaged employees, and advance long-term competitiveness.

One problem with implementing flexible or custom work options can be a lack of clarity about who owns them: line managers? Or hiring managers, benefits managers, or even top managers? Because large organizations are complex and expertise is fragmented, experts recommend that unit, department, or operations managers take a lead and suggest a pilot program or policy.[8] Make it a living experiment, based on trial and error. Be open to mistakes.

Following a pilot test, managers should report the benefits as well as the challenges and solutions for management review and then adjust to inform the next round of experimentation. For example, Cox Communications initiated a "cyber agent" program to relieve overcrowding in its call center. Over a hundred customer service representatives went virtual and worked from home. Some agents, however, did not meet performance expectations, creating the need to rescind their cyber status. It is always wise to check on what is working and adjust accordingly. Similarly, the American Lung Association of California moved workers to remote working from home when asbestos was discovered in its building. Some employees, however, could not work productively at home. For these workers, a safe temporary work site was found while a permanent building was under construction.[9]

Don't wait for a crisis or business-wide plan to implement the idea of custom fit. "Clean up your own backyard," says workplace flexibility author and professor Ellen Ernst Kossek. She advises unit managers to create a microculture that supports diverse ways of working that suit a person's needs while delivering value to the business.[10] Not only can that create a custom fit for employees, it can also catalyze change in the organization more broadly as other units see the benefits.

Executives: Champion New Ways to Work

Sometimes organizational culture change comes from the top because leaders realize it is the right thing to do. Jim Johnson of Johnson Moving and Storage did not intend for work policies at his company to be detrimental to mothers. When he learned that they were, he changed them. Only then did he learn that the changes he made were good for his bottom line. Dean Mary Ann Mason of the University of California at Berkeley conducted research on why, when more women than men were graduating with Ph.D.'s, there were so few women tenured professors. When she uncovered the reason, she encouraged the university to revamp its tenure track and other policies to better accommodate all workers with caregiving responsibilities. Leaders can be powerful catalysts for change.

Don't wait until it's your son or daughter who is torn apart by job and family. If you are a chief executive or other top manager, you can play a pivotal role introducing custom-fit policies. You can model commitment to a flexible workplace and promote an employee-friendly culture of trust, mutual respect, and work-life fit. You can champion customization so that it can become a part of strategic thinking and organizational design, not just a reactive response to a one-time problem.

Brenda Barnes, chief executive of Sara Lee, required her senior staff members to commit to offering "returnships": internships to provide an on-ramp for people interested in returning to the workforce after being out of it for a number of years. Managers let the returnees try different jobs, not necessarily full time, for four to six months, and then gave structured feedback and evaluations. Initially middle managers resisted the program, but Barnes saw the strategic benefit. She insisted that a workforce that mirrored the company's customer demographics was a key competitive advantage and that returnships were a win for both their incumbents and Sara Lee.[11]

For employees of the City of Atlanta, support came from the city's top executive. After virtual work was successfully implemented in the city courts, Mayor Shirley Franklin wanted to expand flexible work options—including job sharing, part-time work, and a compressed workweek—to other departments. Managers worried about scheduling difficulties, the impact on promotions, and security, but they persevered. The result went beyond even Mayor Franklin's initiative; when the HR department struggled to create a compressed schedule for some employees, workers formed a committee and designed their own schedules—in effect, they used a high-commitment, self-managing team to fix the glitch.[12]

Top managers have the unique opportunity to be strong champions leading the effort toward custom-fit workplaces that reach beyond their own work address. Gibbons, a Newark, New Jersey, law firm ranked by *Working Mother* magazine as one of the best law firms for women, found this to be true. Its champion at the top was one of the first female partners. She challenged the firm to become an open, results-based work environment, using virtual work and flexible scheduling to improve the culture and reduce turnover costs. She was right; leaders saw such a strong positive impact on their culture that they began to mentor other organizations to help them reap similar benefits.[13]

Human Resources Professionals: Spur the Dialogue

Leaders in the field of human resources and their professional organizations, such as the Society of Human Resource Management, can make change by facilitating dialogue about the value of custom fit and a flexible workplace. They can showcase model programs and practices at their annual conferences, disseminate templates so companies can easily create guidelines for implementing policies, and direct media attention to companies and leaders whose innovations can be copied by others. They can play a key role in the dissemination and sharing of information so that organizations don't have to reinvent the wheel.

Inside their own organizations, human resources staff can make the business case for workplace flexibility and innovation to a company's leadership. Central to this effort is focusing on the idea of fit instead of balance, according to Cali Yost, author of *Work+Life: Finding the Fit That's Right for You*. Yost tells how, in her experience, business leaders' eyes glaze over when they hear mention of work-life balance, because they equate it with working less. Yes, for some, it is about working less, but "mostly it means working differently, more flexibly, smarter and better."[14] Yost says that leaders finally get it when they realize they themselves have a unique set of personal and job commitments, so others must too. This recognition lends itself to a better understanding that everyone needs a custom fit.

Human resources professionals can serve as an intermediary between management and workers: they can help support implementation by finding out which work arrangements are desired and valuable to company employees, communicating to employees their role in creating the win-win of custom fits, and supporting the process of change as inevitable bumps in the road arise. Further, HR can take successful pilot programs tried in one part of the organization and help implement something similar in other departments.

Human resources can also advocate for performance evaluations that are fit-neutral: that don't penalize a person who makes a lane change, adopts a flexible schedule, or tries another custom-fit option. Few employees (less than one-third) are confident that using a flexible work arrangement won't jeopardize their jobs or careers.[15] Further, a recent study by the consulting firm McKinsey & Company found that just a quarter of companies have performance evaluation systems that neutralize the effects of parental leave or other flexible work options.[16] Clearly there is a leadership role here for the human resources professional who understands the importance of a worker's unique value added, whatever the person's work arrangement looks like.

Public Policy Makers: Speed the Change

Public policy can play an important role in speeding change so that the custom-fit workplace becomes a reality for more people, and sooner. In a country as creative and entrepreneurial as the United States, where organizational adaptations to competitive conditions are usually fast and furious, it is surprising that high-quality custom work arrangements are still the exception: less than half of employers provide access to most types of flexible work options for all or even most of their workers.[17] The United States lags far behind other industrialized nations in support of work-life fit—whether that fit is needed to care for a critically ill family member, to upgrade to needed skills, or to ease into retirement. A recent survey of twenty-one high-income countries found all but one ahead of the U.S. in workplace flexibility. Of the twenty-one countries surveyed, seventeen have laws allowing parents to move to part-time or otherwise adjust their working hours; twelve have laws to help people adjust work schedules for training and education; eleven allow reduced hours prior to full retirement; five allow working time adjustments for family caregiving responsibilities; and five give everyone the right to alternative work arrangements.[18]

The United States has no laws encouraging employers to give workers job flexibility. In other countries, such as the United Kingdom and Australia, workers have a right to request flexible working without being penalized for asking. These "right to request" laws respect that workers need alternative work arrangements for a variety of reasons, not just family caregiving. Because they apply to all workers, they eliminate tensions over flexibility between workers with and without family responsibilities. Employers have the right to refuse requests on business, operational, or organizational grounds, but workers can't be disadvantaged for asking. The laws, quite simply, nudge employers in the direction of flexible working—making it easier for employees to find a custom fit between their job and personal responsibilities.

This was the thinking behind the U.S. Working Families Flexibility Act, a law introduced by the late Senator Edward Kennedy and Congresswoman Carolyn Maloney in December 2007.[19] It sought to give employees a "right to request" alternative work arrangements, without focusing primarily on reduced hours. It recognized that the demand for different work options was going to increase in the future as demographic and technological shifts continue. The bill, however, never became law.

What next, then, to move toward making custom fit standard operating procedure? A major report released recently offers a five-pronged solution. The report was based on a multiyear study of how to bring workplace flexibility to the United States, and was sponsored by Workplace Flexibility 2010, a consensus-building initiative at Georgetown University Law Center.[20] Workplace Flexibility 2010 aims to move beyond old ideas, laws, and ways of working to suggest incentives, supports, and models to make a "new normal" in the American workplace, a normal that takes a comprehensive, state-of-the-art approach to work-life fit. The report concludes that public policy must have five complementary prongs to meet the challenges of the twenty-first century head-on and strategically:

- Support a national communications campaign showing why the U.S. workplace needs to be restructured to support more flexibility to benefit employees, businesses, families, communities, and the nation.
- Provide tools to help employers implement alternative work arrangements, including technical assistance, training, information, and support.
- Invest in on-the-ground experiments in innovative ways to work flexibly, taking stock of lessons learned, and disseminating the knowledge to new industries, employers, and categories of workers.
- Make the federal government a model flexible workplace, transforming it into an example of "the new normal"; lead the national conversation by example about what makes twenty-first-century workplaces work.
- Build partnerships across business, governments, unions, community groups, and other employee and employer groups to carry out the first four prongs and embed new approaches to work into the structure and culture of all workplaces.

Speeding up change is precisely the role of public policy. Government can play an important role in enabling citizens to combine their paycheck jobs with their other personal, family, and civic responsibilities.

Above and Beyond the Bottom Line

The custom-fit work-life strategies described in this book are intended to provide inspiration along with solid information.

Use these models or envision something new. The workplace practices we describe here demonstrate that there are options that work well in very diverse settings, options that are good not only for people but also for businesses. This book is a call to keep the innovation coming.

It's also a call to work together. All of us are still trying to solve the work-life problem individually, whether we spend our days on a manufacturing line, in a cubicle, or even in the White House. We are making it up as we go along, an ineffective human capital strategy for the serious challenges we face. We need collective wisdom and solutions. We need to talk to one another about subjects that make us uncomfortable, like our worry that our jobs might disappear overnight, that overwork compromises our families, and that our lives do not feel quite under control. Lasting change will only come about when everyone from the boardroom to the cashier counter sits down to discuss solutions.

We live in an exciting time, a time when people and organizations have only begun to free themselves from old notions about when, where, and how work should be done. More discoveries lie ahead. We believe that readers of this book will develop new custom-fit workplace practices. To share your story or read those of others, go online to CustomFitWorkplace.org. We look forward to hearing from you.

Notes

Chapter One

1. Vicky Lowell, "No Time to Be Sick: Why Everyone Suffers When Workers Don't Have Paid Sick Leave," Institute for Women's Policy Research, May 2004; retrieved March 15, 2010, from www.iwpr.org/pdf/B242.pdf.
2. Mothers' level of conflict remained around 43 percent. See Ellen Galinsky, Kerstin Aumann, and James T. Bond, "Times Are Changing: Gender and Generation at Work and at Home," Families and Work Institute 2008 National Study of the Changing Workplace, 2009; retrieved February 10, 2010, from www.familiesandwork.org/site/research/reports/Times_Are_Changing.pdf.
3. Deborah Frett, "The Work-Life Tip Sheet: 10 Steps to a Successful Workplace," October 22, 2009; retrieved February 10, 2010, from www.huffingtonpost.com/deborah-frett/the-work-life-tip-sheet-1_b_329975.html.
4. National Alliance for Caregiving and AARP, "Caregiving in the U.S.: Findings from the National Caregiver Survey" (Executive Summary), April 2004; retrieved March 15, 2010, from www.caregiving.org/data/04execsumm.pdf.
5. Fran Durekas, "Working Parents," *BusinessWeek*, September 21, 2009; retrieved February 10, 2010, from www.businessweek.com/careers/workingparents/blog/archives/2009/09/_a_changing_wor.html.
6. In fact, smart phone technology will accelerate the globalization we are currently witnessing firsthand. Not

dependent on land-line cable, developing countries are adopting cell phone use rapidly. And smart phone technology is reported to be "ramping faster than any tech cycle" in modern times (Jefferson Graham, "Web 2.0 Speakers See Mobile Takeover in Future," *USA Today*, October 22, 2009, p. 7B). This means that globalization will accelerate.

7. Life Meets Work, "Studies: It's the Fall of Our Employees' Discontent," November 17, 2009; retrieved February 10, 2010, from www.workforce.com/section/00/article/26/81/68 .php.

8. Jodie Levin-Epstein, "Getting Punched: The Job and Family Clock," Center for Law and Social Policy (CLASP), July 2006, pp. 4–5; retrieved March 15, 2010, from www.clasp .org/admin/site/publications/files/0303.pdf.

9. Judy Casey and Karen Corday, "Work-Life Fit and the Life Course: An Interview with Phyllis Moen," Sloan Work and Family Research Network, *Network News* 11, no. 9 (September 2009); retrieved February 10, 2010, from http:// wfnetwork.bc.edu/The_Network_News/63/experts.htm.

10. P. Moen, E. Kelly, and R. Huang, "'Fit' Inside the Work/ Family Black Box: An Ecology of the Life Course, Cycles of Control Reframing." *Journal of Occupational and Organizational Psychology* 81 (2008): 411–433. See also Casey and Corday, "Work-Life Fit and the Life Course."

11. Joan included a chapter on flexible work approaches in her 2006 book, co-authored with Kristin Rowe-Finkbeiner, *The Motherhood Manifesto* (New York: Nations Books, 2006).

12. Casey and Corday, "Work-Life Fit and the Life Course."

13. In some cases we have changed names, altered noncritical details, or described composite people to protect privacy.

Chapter Two

1. Jodie Levin-Epstein, "Getting Punched: The Job and Family Clock," Center for Law and Social Policy (CLASP), July

2006; retrieved March 15, 2010, from www.clasp.org/admin/site/publications/files/0303.pdf.

2. Corporate Voices for Working Families, "Business Impacts of Flexibility: An Imperative for Expansion," Washington, D.C.: November 2005, pp. 14–15.

3. M. Thompson, *Hay Report: Compensation and Benefits Strategies for 2000 and Beyond* (Philadelphia: The Hay Group, January 25, 2000).

4. Jennifer E. Swanberg, Jacquelyn B. James, and Sharon P. McKechnie, "Can Business Benefit by Providing Workplace Flexibility to Hourly Workers?" Issue Brief No. 3, CitySales Study, p. 2; retrieved February 17, 2010, from www.citisalesstudy.com/hourly-ib3_bc_flex.html.

5. Resource managers: see Joan Williams, *Unbending Gender: Why Work and Family Conflict and What to Do About It* (New York: Oxford University Press, 2000, p. 85). U.S. workers: see A Better Balance, "The Business Case for Workplace Flexibility," March 2008; retrieved February 17, 2010, from http://abetterbalance.org/cms/index2.php?option=com_docman&task=doc_view&gid=24&Itemid=99999999.

6. A. Marzolini, *Moving Forward 2001: The Experiences and Attitudes of Executive Women in Canada* (Toronto, Ontario: Pollara, 2001).

7. Catalyst, *Two Careers, One Marriage: Making It Work in the Workplace* (New York: Catalyst, 1997).

8. The Conference Board, "U.S. Job Satisfaction at Lowest Level in Two Decades," January 5, 2010; retrieved February 17, 2010, from www.conference-board.org/utilities/press Detail.cfm?press_ID=3820.

9. Levin-Epstein, "Getting Punched: The Job and Family Clock," p. 8.

10. Corporate Voices for Working Families, "Business Impacts of Flexibility."

11. Ashley Acker, "The Business Case for Workplace Flexibility," Ezine articles, 2009; retrieved February 17, 2010, from http://EzineArticles.com/?expert=Ashley_Acker, Ph.D.

12. J. S. Arthur, "Seeking Equilibrium," *Human Resource Executive* 15, no. 7 (2001): 34–38.

13. John Helyar and Ann Harrington, "The Only Company Wal-Mart Fears: Nobody Runs Warehouse Clubs Better Than Costco, Where Shoppers Can't Resist Luxury Products at Bargain Prices," *Fortune*, November 24, 2003.

14. R. Pruchno, L. Litchfield, and M. Fried, "Measuring the Impact of Workplace Flexibility," Boston: Boston College, Center for Work & Family, 2000.

15. D. A. Wilburn, "The 100 Best Companies for Working Mothers," *Working Mother*, October 1998.

16. James T. Bond, Cynthia Thompson, Ellen Galinsky, and David Prottas, "Highlights of the National Study of the Changing Workforce: Work-Life Supports on the Job," New York: Families and Work Institute, 2002, p. 14; retrieved March 15, 2010, from www.familiesandwork.org/site/work/workforce/2002nscw.html.

17. Amy Richman, Arlene Johnson, and Lisa Buxbaum, "Workplace Flexibility for Low Wage Workers," Washington, D.C.: Corporate Voices for Working Families, October 2006, p. 16.

18. Swanberg, James, and McKechnie, "Can Business Benefit by Providing Workplace Flexibility to Hourly Workers?" p. 2.

19. Retention: see J. Glass and S. B. Estes, "The Family Responsive Workplace," *Annual Review of Sociology* 23 (1997): 289–313. Return: see Janet C. Gornick and Marcia K. Meyers, *Families That Work: Policies for Reconciling Parenthood and Employment* (New York: Russell Sage Foundation, 2003), p. 245.

20. Profitability: see J. Oakley, "Linking Organizational Characteristics to Employee Attitudes and Behavior—A

Look at the Downstream Effects on Market Response and Financial Performance," Forum for People Performance Management & Measurement, Evanston, Ill.: Northwestern University, 2005. Shareholder return: see "Human Capital Index: Linking Human Capital and Shareholder Value, 2000," Watson Wyatt Worldwide; retrieved February 17, 2010, from www.watsonwyatt.com/us/research/resrender .asp?id=EU21&page=1.

21. Jean Flatley McGuire, Kaitlyn Kenny, and Phillis Brashler, "Flexible Work Arrangements: The Fact Sheet," Workplace Flexibility 2010, Georgetown University Law Center, p. 7; retrieved February 17, 2010, from www.law.georgetown .edu/workplaceflexibility2010/definition/general/FWA _FactSheet.pdf.

22. A. Konrad and R. Mangel, "The Impact of Work-Life Programs on Firm Productivity," *Strategic Management Journal* 21 (2000): 1225–1237.

23. Acker, "The Business Case for Workplace Flexibility," and Swanberg, James, and McKechnie, "Can Business Benefit by Providing Workplace Flexibility to Hourly Workers?" p. 3.

24. Richman, Johnson, and Buxbaum, "Workplace Flexibility for Low Wage Workers," p. 16.

25. Swanberg, James, and McKechnie, "Can Business Benefit by Providing Workplace Flexibility to Hourly Workers?" p. 3.

26. Claire Shipman and Katty Kay, *Womenomics* (New York: Harper Business, 2009), pp. 2–4.

27. Watson Wyatt, "Watson Wyatt Human Capital Index: Human Capital as a Lead Indicator of Shareholder Value," Watson Wyatt, 2006; retrieved February 17, 2010, from www.watsonwyatt.com/research/resrender.asp?id=W -488&page=3.

28. B. E. Becker and M. A. Huselid, "Human Resources Strategies, Complementaries, and Firm Performance," 1998;

retrieved February 17, 2010, from http://mgt.buffalo.edu/departments/ohr/becker/publications/HumanResources Strategies.pdf.

29. Corporate Voices for Working Families, "Business Impacts of Flexibility," pp. 14–15.

30. McGuire, Kenny, and Brashler, "Flexible Work Arrangements," p. 7.

31. McGuire, Kenny, and Brashler, "Flexible Work Arrangements," p. 7.

32. "Chubb Workplace Flexibility Initiative Boosts Employee Productivity," Chubb Press Release, July 18, 2005.

33. "Questions and Answers About Telework: A Sloan Work and Family Research Network Fact Sheet," p. 3; retrieved February 17, 2010, from http://wfnetwork.bc.edu/pdfs/telework.pdf.

34. WFC Resources, "Making the Business Case for Flexibility," June 2006, UpDate Column, Minnetonka, Minn. See also: Corporate Voices for Working Families, "Business Impacts of Flexibility," pp. 14–15.

35. WFC Resources, "Making the Business Case for Flexibility."

36. Corporate Voices for Working Families, "Business Impacts of Flexibility," pp. 14–15.

37. Devin Dwyer, "Can a Flexible Boss Improve Your Health?" ABC News, October 14, 2009; retrieved February 17, 2010, from http://abcnews.go.com/Health/study-flexible-boss-workplace-means-healthier-employees-families/story?id=8819760.

38. Ellen Galinsky, "Wellness Is the Responsibility of Business as Well as Worker," Huffington Post, September 22, 2009, retrieved February 17, 2010, from www.huffingtonpost.com/ellen-galinsky/wellness-is-the-responsib_b_291500.html.

39. Kelleen Kay and David Gray, "The Stress of Balancing Work and Family: The Impact on Parent and Child Health and the Need for Workplace Flexibility," Research Paper—The Next Social Contract, New America Foundation,

October 2007, pp. 8–9, retrieved February 17, 2010, from www.newamerica.net/publications/policy/stress _balancing_work_and_family.

40. Gornick and Meyers, *Families That Work,* pp. 245–246.
41. Sylvia Ann Hewlett, "Flexible Work Arrangements: A Smart Strategy in Troubled Times," Forbes.com, May 15, 2009; retrieved February 17, 2010, from www.forbes .com/2009/05/15/work-life-balance-forbes-woman-leader ship-flextime_print.html.
42. Green Houston, "Sustainability Projects—Fuels, Vehicles, and Transit"; retrieved March 10, 2010, from www .greenhoustontx.gov/epr-fuels.html.
43. J. E. Perry-Smith and T. C. Blum, "Work-Family Human Resource Bundles and Perceived Organizational Performance," *Academy of Management Journal* 43 (2000): 1107–1117.

Chapter Three

1. Eyal Press, "Family-Leave Values," *New York Times,* July 29, 2007; retrieved February 18, 2010, from www.nytimes .com/2007/07/29/magazine/29discrimination-t .html?pagewanted=1&_r=1&ref=magazine'.
2. Case study from Boston College Center for Work & Family, "Overcoming the Implementation Gap: How 20 Leading Companies Are Making Flexibility Work," Boston College, Chestnut Hill, Mass. Note: Raytheon extended the offer of compressed workweeks to its unionized hourly employees as well. To date, the union has not accepted the offer to participate.
3. E-mail interview with Anne Palmer, December 8, 2009.
4. Note: We are intentional in using *reduced workload* in place of *part-time* as the umbrella term here to connote a reduction of work responsibilities commensurate with the reduction in hours and pay for both hourly and full-time workers.

5. Boston College Center for Work & Family, "Overcoming the Implementation Gap," p. 54.

6. Jennifer Turano, "Two Workers, Wearing One Hat," *New York Times*, October 3, 2009; retrieved February 18, 2010, from www.nytimes.com/2009/10/04/jobs/04pre.html?scp=1&sq=two%20workers%20wearing%20one%20hat&st=cse.

7. Boston College Center for Work & Family, "Overcoming the Implementation Gap."

8. Boston College Center for Work & Family, "Overcoming the Implementation Gap, p. 80.

9. Eve Nicholas, "Want a Job-Share Position? How to Land One," HeraldNet.com, March 5, 2008; retrieved February 18, 2010, from www.heraldnet.com/article/20080305/BIZ/72327084.

10. The Balancing Act, "Telework: Part of the Work-Life Balance Equation," Employment Policy Foundation, March 11, 2004; retrieved March 21, 2010, from http://wfnetwork.bc.edu/downloads/EPF/EPF_Telework.pdf.

11. Matt Williams, "Swine Flu: Is Government Ready to Telework?" Government Technology, April 28, 2009; retrieved February 18, 2010, from www.govtech.com/gt/articles/649394.

12. It is worth noting that the 9/80 schedule put into use at Raytheon was discussed with the unionized, hourly employees. The union has consistently declined to participate in the 9/80 scheduling program, perhaps based on fear of lost overtime income.

13. S. Lambert, "Making a Difference for Hourly Employees." In *Work-Life Policies That Make a Real Difference for Individuals, Families, and Organizations*, edited by A. Booth and A. Crouter (Washington, D.C.: Urban Institute Press, 2009), pp. 169–196.

14. Work Life Law Center, "Union Members and FRD," n.d.; retrieved February 18, 2010, from www.worklifelaw.org/UnionMembersFRD.html.

15. Labor Project for Working Families, "Flex Pack: A Toolkit on Organizing, Bargaining and Legislating for Worker-Controlled Flexibility," n.d.; retrieved February 18, 2010, from www.working-families.org/learnmore/pdf/flexpack.pdf.
16. Lambert, "Making a Difference for Hourly Employees."
17. Punithavathi, Srikant and Doris Rajakumari John, "Human Resource Management Case Study: Costco's Employee Loyalty Strategies," IBS Research Center, 2008.
18. Lambert, "Making a Difference for Hourly Employees."
19. Philip Moss and others, "When Firms Restructure: Understanding Work-Life Outcomes," in *Work and Life Integration in Organizations: New Directions for Theory and Practice*, edited by E. Kossek and S. Lambert (Mahwah, N.J.: Erlbaum, 2005), pp. 127–150.
20. Lambert, "Making a Difference for Hourly Employees."
21. Bill Stanczykiewicz, "Savvy Businesses Friendly to Families," *Indianapolis Star*, September 1, 2008.
22. Jeffrey Pfeffer, "Human Resources from an Organizational Behavior Perspective: Some Paradoxes Explained," *Journal of Economic Perspectives* 21, no. 4 (2007): 115.
23. Hewitt Associates, "Hewitt Survey Suggests U.S. Companies Not Effectively Managing Workplace Flexibility Programs," *BusinessWire*, April 30, 2008.
24. Sue Shellenbarger, "Does Avoiding a 9-to-5 Grind Make You a Target for Layoffs?" *Wall Street Journal*, April 22, 2009; retrieved February 18, 2010, from http://online.wsj.com/article/SB124036041384541497.html.
25. Sylvia Ann Hewlett, *Off-Ramps and On-Ramps: Keeping Talented Women on the Road to Success* (Boston: Harvard University Press, 2007), p. 32.
26. Equally Shared Parenting Real-Life Stories, "Ben and Alicia," 2007; retrieved February 18, 2010, from http://equallysharedparenting.com/RealLifeStories.htm.

27. Sylvia Ann Hewlett and Carolyn Buck Luce, "Off-Ramps and On-Ramps: Keeping Talented Women on the Road to Success," *Harvard Business Review*, March 2005.

28. Boston College Center for Work & Family, "Overcoming the Implementation Gap," p. 9.

29. Boston College Center for Work & Family, "Overcoming the Implementation Gap," p. 11.

30. Joan Blades and Kristin Rowe-Finkbeiner, *The Motherhood Manifesto: What America's Moms Want—and What to Do About It* (New York: Nation Books, 2006).

31. James Johnson, "Talent Troubles: How to Attract and Keep Good People and Control Costs," April 22, 2008. Information used with permission from James Johnson, from his 2008 presentation on flexibility.

32. Ken Giglio, "Workplace Flexibility Case Studies," Sloan Work and Family Research Network, n.d.; retrieved February 18, 2010, from http://wfnetwork.bc.edu/template .php?name=casestudy.

Chapter Four

1. WorldatWork, "Telework Trendlines 2009," data collected by The Dieringer Research Group Inc., February 2009; retrieved February 19, 2010, from www.workingfromany where.org/news/Trendlines_2009.pdf.

2. See B. Wiesenfeld, S. Raghuram, and R. Garud, "Organizational Identification Among Virtual Workers: The Role of Need for Affiliation and Work-Based Social Support," *Journal of Management* 27 (2001): 213–229. Also see C. U. Grosse, "Managing Communication with Virtual Intercultural Teams," *Business Communication Quarterly* 65, no. 4 (2002): 22–38.

3. Hudson Employment Index, "Home and Office—Workers Want It All," July 19, 2006; retrieved March 20, 2010, from http://us.hudson.com/node.asp?kwd=survey-2006-archive.

4. U.S. House of Representatives, Committee on Education and the Workforce. "Telework: The Impact on Workplace Policy in the U.S." Hearing, October 28, 1999. Washington, D.C.: Government Printing Office, 1999.

5. The Telework Coalition, "Telework Facts," n.d.; retrieved February 19, 2010, from www.telcoa.org/id33.htm.

6. "Teleworking Increases Productivity and Morale, Saves Money," Government Technology, July 6, 2005; retrieved February 19, 2010, from www.govtech.com/gt/print_article .php?id=94557.

7. U.S. Environmental Protection Agency, "Telework Programs: Implementing Commuter Benefits as One of the Nation's Best Workplaces for Commuters," January 2005; retrieved March 12, 2010, from www.gpoaccess.gov/ harvesting/telework.pdf.

8. EKOS Research Associates, "Canadians and Working from Home," May 2001; retrieved February 19, 2010, from www .ekos.ca/admin/press_releases/telework4.pdf; WorldatWork, "Telework Trendlines 2009."

9. Steven R. Rayner, "The Virtual Team Challenge," 1997; retrieved February 19, 2010, from http://raynerassoc.com/ Resources/Virtual.pdf.

10. Richard Hart, "Robots Changing the Face of Telecommuting," KGO/ABC News Report aired November 8, 2009; retrieved February 19, 2010, from http://abclocal.go.com/kgo/ story?section=news/drive_to_discover&id=7107120.

11. WorldatWork, "Telework Trendlines 2009."

12. "Management by Walking About," Economist, September 8, 2008; available by subscription at www.economist .com/businessfinance/management/displayStory.cfm ?story_id=12075015&source=login.

13. John Halamka, "How I Learned to Stop Worrying and Love Telecommuting," CIO.com, March 17, 2008; retrieved February 19, 2010, from www.cio.com/article/197800/

How_I_Learned_to_Stop_Worrying_and_Love
_Telecommuting.

14. Faris Yamini, Hari Balakrishnan, Giao Nguyen, and Xavier Lopez, "Real-Time Collaborative Technologies: Incentives and Impediments," retrieved February 19, 2010, from www -inst.eecs.berkeley.edu/~eecsba1/sp97/reports/eecsba1d/ report/.

15. Jennifer McAdams, "1-800 Contacts Fine-Tuning a Sales Strategy," *Computerworld,* September 18, 2006; retrieved February 19, 2010, from www.computerworld.com/s/ article/112785/Fine_tuning_a_Sales_Strategy.

16. Midwest Institute for Telecommuting Education, "Strategic Telework Research in Disability Employment Final Report Developing and Implementing Strategies for Employing Teleworkers with Disabilities," March 31, 2008; retrieved February 19, 2010, from www.mite.org/STRIDE%20 Final%20Report.pdf.

17. Midwest Institute for Telecommuting Education, "Strategic Telework Research in Disability Employment Final Report."

18. Ravi S. Gajendran and David A. Harrison, "The Good, the Bad, and the Unknown About Telecommuting: Meta-Analysis of Psychological Mediators and Individual Consequences," *Journal of Applied Psychology* 92, no. 6 (2007), 1524–1541.

19. Gajendran and Harrison, "The Good, the Bad, and the Unknown About Telecommuting."

20. U.S. Environmental Protection Agency, "Telework Programs: Implementing Commuter Benefits as One of the Nation's Best Workplaces for Commuters," June 2007; retrieved March 15, 2010, from www.bestworkplaces.org/ pdf/carpool_June07.pdf.

21. Billie Williamson, "Managing Remote Workers," *Business-Week,* July 16, 2009; retrieved February 19, 2010, from www.businessweek.com/magazine/content/09_30/

b4140064520044.htm?chan=magazine+channel_personal+business.

Chapter Five

1. Shelly Correll, Stephen Benard, and In Paik, "Getting a Job: Is There a Motherhood Penalty?" *American Journal of Sociology* 1297 (2007): 112.
2. Sylvia Ann Hewlett and Carolyn Buck Luce, "Off-Ramps and On-Ramps: Keeping Talented Women and the Road to Success," *Harvard Business Review* and Center for Work-Life Policy, February 28, 2005.
3. Cathleen Benko and Anne Benko, *Mass Career Customization: Aligning the Workplace with Today's Nontraditional Workforce* (Boston: Harvard Business School Press: 2007), p. 82.
4. Hema Krishnan, "Combat Turnover Among Executive Women," Working Mother, November 2, 2009; retrieved February 20, 2010, from www.workingmother.com/BestCompanies/women-in-business/2009/11/combat-turnover-among-executive-women.
5. For more information on the 2001 and subsequent Pepperdine studies on women and profitability see Roy D. Adler, "Profit, Thy Name Is . . . Woman?" February 27, 2009, Miller-McCune.com. Retrieved March 23, 2010, from www.miller-mccune.com/business-economics/profit-thy-name-is-woman-3920/.
6. Hannah Seligson, "Off Ramp to On Ramp: It Can Be a Hard Journey," *New York Times*, December 6, 2008; retrieved February 20, 2010, from www.nytimes.com/2008/12/07/jobs/07return.html.
7. J. W. Curtis, "Balancing Work and Family for Faculty," *Academe* 90, no. 6 (2004), 21–23.
8. Stefan Sagmeister, "The Power of Time Off," October 2009; retrieved February 20, 2010, from www.ted.com/talks/stefan_sagmeister_the_power_of_time_off.html.

9. Shelly K. Schwartz, "The Corporate Sabbatical," CNN Money, November 15, 1999; retrieved February 20, 2010, from http://money.cnn.com/1999/11/15/life/q_sabbatical/.

10. Boston College Center for Work & Family, "Overcoming the Implementation Gap: How 20 Leading Companies Are Making Flexibility Work," Boston College, Chestnut Hill, Mass., p. 96.

11. Boston College Center for Work & Family, "Overcoming the Implementation Gap," p. 98.

12. Seligson, "Off Ramp to On Ramp."

13. Seligson, "Off Ramp to On Ramp."

14. Maureen Clarke, "Coaching Moms Back to Work," Blueprint Group Reading Room, n.d.; retrieved February 20, 2010, from www.blueprintgroup.ca/readingroom_articles_backto work.htm.

15. Pamela Weinsaft, "Goldman Sachs Returnship (SM) Program Helps Top Women On-Ramp into Finance," Glass Hammer, September 23, 2009; retrieved February 20, 2010, from www.theglasshammer.com/news/2009/09/23/goldman -sachs-returnshipsm-program-helps-top-women-on-ramp -into-finance/.

16. Sarah Webb, "Returning to Science," *Science Careers Magazine*, October 30, 2009; retrieved February 20, 2010, from http://sciencecareers.sciencemag.org/career_magazine/ previous_issues/articles/2009_10_30/caredit.a0900133.

17. Karie Frasch, Mary Ann Mason, Angy Stacy, Marc Goulden, and Carol Hoffman, "Creating a Family Friendly Department: Chairs and Deans Toolkit," July 1, 2007, Berkeley, Calif.: UC Faculty Family Friendly Edge. Retrieved March 22, 2010, from http://ucfamilyedge.berkeley.edu/toolkit.html.

18. Frasch, Mason, Stacy, Goulden, and Hoffman, "Creating a Family Friendly Department," p. 4.

19. iRelaunch, "iRelaunch's Comprehensive List of Career Reentry Programs Worldwide," July 2009; retrieved February 20, 2010, from www.irelaunch.com/docs/complist.pdf.

20. Sue Shellenbarger, "Getting from At-Home to On-the-Job, Even Now," *Wall Street Journal*, July 29, 2009; retrieved February 20, 2010, from http://online.wsj.com/article/SB10001424052970204563304574316540263060898.html.

21. Elizabeth, Garone, "Pile On Mentors in Tough Times," *Wall Street Journal*, October 6, 2009; retrieved February 20, 2010, from http://online.wsj.com/article/SB10001424052748703298004574455172409504420.html.

Chapter Six

1. Paul Davidson, "Contract Workers Swelling Ranks," *USA Today*, December 6, 2009; retrieved February 20, 2010, from http://m.usatoday.com/home/1120885/1/.

2. Prashant Gopal, "Now Hiring: Contract Workers?" *Business-Week*, June 30, 2009; retrieved February 20, 2010, from www.businessweek.com/print/managing/content/jun2009/ca20090630_912379.htm.

3. Davidson, "Contract Workers Swelling Ranks."

4. Veritude, "The New Normal: Recession Response and Workforce Planning," Attitude Measurement Corporation, 2009; retrieved February 20, 2010, from www1.vtrenz.net/imarkownerfiles/ownerassets/1010/ReportRd11.pdf.

5. Teresa Garcia, "Growing Trend of Temporary Executives," KGO/ABC News, March 3, 2009; retrieved February 20, 2010, from http://abclocal.go.com/kgo/story?section=news/business&id=6686066&pt=print.

6. Davidson, "Contract Workers Swelling Ranks."

7. "Talent on Tap: The Fashion for Hiring Temps Has Reached the Executive Suite," *Economist*, December 10, 2009; retrieved February 20, 2010, from www.economist.com/businessfinance/displaystory.cfm?story_id=15064293.

8. Morra Aarons-Mele, "Jumping Back on the Ladder: Talking with Harvard's Christine Heenan," Huffington Post, July 30, 2009; retrieved March 15, 2010, from

www.huffingtonpost.com/morra-aaronsmele/jumping-back
-on-the-ladde_b_220888.html.

9. Sue Shellenbarger, "How Stay-at-Home Moms Are Filling an Executive Niche," *Wall Street Journal*, April 30, 2008; retrieved February 20, 2010, from http://online.wsj.com/ article/SB120951025037054311.html?mod=pj_main _hs_coll.

10. Life Meets Work and Ask Liz Ryan, "Work/Life Issues in America" (white paper); available with sign-up at http:// www.lifemeetswork.com/pages/template2.asp?pageID= 193.

11. See also Garcia, "Growing Trend of Temporary Executives."

12. "The World of Work," *Economist*, January 4, 2007.

13. Debbie Fledderjohann, "Baby Boomers and Contracting," Top Echelon Contracting, June 11, 2008; retrieved February 20, 2010, from www.topecheloncontracting.com/recruiters/ Detail.aspx?at=3&aid=48.

14. "The 2006 Merrill Lynch New Retirement Study" builds on the work of the "2005 Merrill Lynch New Retirement Survey," offering a good glimpse into the trends of Baby Boomers on the verge of retirement. Retrieved March 23, 2010, from www.ml.com/media/66482.pdf.

15. Garcia, "Growing Trend of Temporary Executives."

16. Louis Uchitelle, "Labor Data Show Surge in Hiring of Temp Workers," *New York Times*, December 20, 2009; retrieved March 20, 2010, from www.nytimes.com/2009/12/21/ business/economy/21temps.html?_r=1.

17. MetLife Mature Market Institute and the Caregiving Alliance, "The MetLife Caregiving Cost Study: Productivity Losses to U.S. Business," July 2006; retrieved February 20, 2010, from www.caregiving.org/data/Caregiver%20Cost %20Study.pdf.

18. Garcia, "Growing Trend of Temporary Executives."

19. See www.topecheloncontracting.com for more on how these type of firms are marketing to clients looking for temporary placement of highly qualified workers.
20. "Talent on Tap."

Chapter Seven

1. Interview with Carla Moquin, founder of Babies At Work, November, 2009. More information available at www.babiesatwork.org/.
2. Ginny Sprang, Mary Secret, and Judith Bradford, "Blending Work and Family: A Case Study," *AFFILIA* 14, no. 1 (Spring 1999): 98–116.
3. Tiffany Sharples, "Bringing Babies to Work." *Time*, January 3, 2008; retrieved February 21, 2010, from www.time.com/time/magazine/article/0,9171,1699879,00.html.
4. Cate Colburn-Smith and Andrea Serrette, *The Milk Memos: How Real Moms Learned to Mix Business with Babies—and How You Can, Too* (New York: Tarcher, 2007), p. 21.
5. Jon P. Weimer, "The Economic Benefits of Breastfeeding: A Review and Analysis," Food and Rural Economics Division, Economic Research Service, U.S. Department of Agriculture, Food Assistance and Nutrition Report, Report No. 13 (Washington, D.C.: U.S. Department of Agriculture, March 2001); retrieved February 21, 2010, from www.ers.usda.gov/publications/fanrr13/fanrr13.pdf.
6. Centers for Disease Control and Prevention, "Breastfeeding Among U.S. Children Born 1999–2006, CDC National Immunization Survey," updated October 20, 2009; retrieved February 21, 2010, from www.cdc.gov/BREASTFEEDING/DATA/NIS_data/.
7. Aist also told us that in her professional experience she has seen many mothers of premature babies forced to return to

work before their babies were even discharged from the newborn intensive care unit.

8. Carla Moquin, *Babies at Work: Bringing New Life to the Workplace*, (Salt Lake City: Carla Moquin, 2008).

9. Sprang, Secret, and Bradford, "Blending Work and Family."

10. Moquin, "Babies at Work."

11. Sprang, Secret, and Bradford, "Blending Work and Family."

Chapter Eight

1. Interview conducted November 17, 2009.

2. John Schmitt, "Unions and Upward Mobility for Service Sector Workers," Center for Economic and Policy Research, April, 2009. According to the study, data from the Current Population Survey (CPS) show that unionization increases service sector employees' wages by 10.1 percent compared to nonunion workers in the same jobs. Unionization also increases the prevalence of benefits like health insurance and pensions for service sector workers. The report also notes that workers with service jobs benefit as much from unionization as workers with manufacturing jobs.

3. "Union Members—2009," Bureau of Labor Statistics news release, January 22, 2010; retrieved February 21, 2010, from www.bls.gov/news.release/pdf/union2.pdf.

4. E-mail interview, December 13, 2009.

5. John Schmitt and Kris Warner, "The Changing Face of Labor, 1983–2008," Center for Economic Policy Research, November 2009; retrieved February 21, 2010, from http://www.cepr.net/index.php/publications/reports/changing-face-of-labor/.

6. Tula Connell, "The Revolution Will Be Twittered" on AFLCIO blog, September 17, 2009; retrieved February 21, 2010, from http://blog.aflcio.org/2009/09/17/the-revolution-will-be-twittered/print/.

7. Vibhuti Mehra, "The Changing Workplace: Union Women Build Power," *Labor Family News*, Winter 2010; retrieved February 21, 2010, from www.working-families.org/new sletter/LPWFNewswebWinter10.pdf.

8. Holly Rosenkrantz, "Trumka Has Detractors, Not Opponents, in AFL-CIO Bid," Bloomberg.com Updates, June 8, 2009; retrieved February 21, 2010, from www.bloomberg.com/apps/news?pid=20601109&sid=aXDR8281bQlw.

9. Shuler, at thirty-nine, is also the youngest person ever to hold such a high position in the labor movement.

10. Phone interview, January 11, 2010.

11. Parija Bhatnagar, "Wal-Mart Seeks to 'Organize' Labor Its Own Way," CNNMoney.com, April 25, 2006; retrieved February 21, 2010, from http://money.cnn.com/2006/04/25/news/companies/walmart_labor/index.htm.

12. Labor Project for Working Families, "Flex Pack: A Toolkit on Organizing, Bargaining and Legislating for Worker -Controlled Flexibility," n.d.; retrieved February 18, 2010, from www.working-families.org/learnmore/pdf/flexpack.pdf.

13. For more information on the Family and Medical Leave Act see Department of Labor, www.dol.gov/whd/fmla/index .htm; access date February 22, 2010.

14. Labor Project for Working Families, "Flex Pack."

15. Jenifer MacGillvary, with Netsy MacGillvary, "Family-Friendly Workplaces: Do Unions Make a Difference?" U.C. Berkeley Labor Center and Labor Project for Working Families, July 2009.

16. Sharon Johnson, "Unions' Appeal to Women Includes Caregiving Help," Women's eNews, May 13, 2008; retrieved February 21, 2010, from www.womensenews.org/article .cfm?aid=3599.

Chapter Nine

1. According to interviews with HPWP Consulting, Ken Bingham's early research showed that other companies

using these practices included Dow Chemical, Lincoln Electric, Merck, 3M, Elkay, Motorola, Hewlett-Packard, and Johnson & Johnson.

2. Richard E. Walton, "From Control to Commitment in the Workplace," in *Human Resource Management: Critical Perspectives on Business and Management,* edited by Michael Poole (New York: Routledge, 1999), p. 18.

3. "Workplace Survey Reveals High Level of Commitment Among Yale Staff" (press release), Yale University Office of Public Affairs, March 6, 2009; retrieved February 21, 2010, from http://opa.yale.edu/news/article.aspx?id=6459&f=34.

4. HPWP Consulting materials and white paper. Sue Bingham, "Reducing Turnover with High Performance Hiring Teams," Rome, Ga.: HPWP Consulting, LLC., 2009.

5. CultureRx, "Business Case," Saint Paul, Minn.: CultureRx, 2009; retrieved March 22, 2010, from http://gorowe.com/wordpress/wp-content/uploads/2009/12/ROWE_Business_Case.pdf. For more information on taking a company in the Results-Only Work Environment direction, see www.gorowe.com.

6. Bingham, "Reducing Turnover with High Performance Hiring Teams."

7. Phone Interview with Sue Bingham and Annie Snowbarger of HPWP Consulting, January 20, 2010.

8. Phone Interview with Sue Bingham and Annie Snowbarger of HPWP Consulting, January 20, 2010.

9. Sue Bingham, "Overview," Rome, Ga.: HPWP Consulting, LLC, 2009.

10. Case studies of Southeastern Mills and Beaulieu of America provided by HPWP Consulting and used with permission of the companies.

11. Cali Ressler and Jody Thompson, *Why Work Sucks and How to Fix It: No Schedules, No Meetings, No Joke—the Simple Change That Can Make Your Job Terrific* (New York: Portfolio, 2008), p. 4.

12. Michelle Conlin, "Smashing the Clock," *Business Week*, December 11, 2006, p. 60.
13. Ressler and Thompson, *Why Work Sucks and How to Fix It.*
14. Though the creators of ROWE assert the program works for all types of workers, retail included, neither of the pilot programs featured here involved retail workers.
15. Conlin, "Smashing the Clock."
16. Boston College Center for Work & Family, "Overcoming the Implementation Gap: How 20 Leading Companies Are Making Flexibility Work," Boston College, Chestnut Hill, Mass.
17. Adrienne Fox, "Gap Outlet: Second Retailer Adopts Results-Only Work Environment Strategy," Society for Human Resource Management, September 8, 2009; available with registration at www.shrm.org/Pages/login.aspx?ReturnUrl=%2fhrdisciplines%2forgempdev%2farticles%2fPages%2fGapOutletROWE.aspx.
18. CultureRx, "Business Case."
19. Fox, "Gap Outlet."
20. CultureRx, "Business Case."
21. Phyllis Moen and Erin L. Kelly, "Flexible Work and Well-Being Study." Flexible Work and Well-Being Center, University of Minnesota, 2007.

Chapter Ten

1. "100 Best Companies to Work for, 2010," Fortune, n.d.; retrieved March 15, 2010, from http://money.cnn.com/magazines/fortune/bestcompanies/2010/.
2. "100 Best Companies to Work for, 2010."
3. The trend in job dissatisfaction was *not* attributable to the economic recession and unemployment rate. Workers under age twenty-five had the highest level of dissatisfaction ever recorded by The Conference Board. See John M. Gibbons, "I Can't Get No . . . Job Satisfaction, That Is," January 2010;

retrieved February 22, 2010, from www.conference-board
.org/publications/describe.cfm?id=1727; and "Americans
Growing Increasingly Unhappy at Work, Survey Finds,"
January 6, 2010; retrieved February 22, 2010, from www
.worldatwork.org/waw/adimComment?id=35985.

4. Stephanie Armour, "U.S. Workers Feel Burn of Long Hours,
Less Leisure," *USA Today*, December 18, 2003; retrieved
February 22, 2010, from http://www.usatoday.com/money/
workplace/2003-12-16-hours-cover_x.htm. Armour cites
study by Families and Work Institute.

5. "Growth Company Executives Want Government Help to
Drive Corporate Innovation," Ernst & Young, December 7,
2009; retrieved February 22, 2010, from www.ey.com/US/
en/Newsroom/News-releases/Growth-company
-executives-want-government-help-to-drive-corporate
-innovation-according-to-Ernst_Young-survey.

6. According to a study conducted by the staffing firm Robert
Half International. Ann Bednarz, "Gas Prices Alter Work
Environment," Network World, June 3, 2008; retrieved
February 22, 2010, from www.cio.com/article/380563/
Gas_Prices_Alter_Work_Environment.

7. Ellen Galinsky, James T. Bond, and E. Jeffrey Hill, "When
Work Works: A Status Report on Workplace Flexibility.
Who Has It? Who Wants It? What Difference Does It
Make?" Families and Work Institute, 2004, p. 21; retrieved
February 22, 2010, from http://familiesandwork.org/3w/
research/downloads/status.pdf; and "Study: For Men, Family
Comes First," *Harvard University Gazette*, May 4, 2000;
retrieved February 22, 2010, from www.news.harvard.edu/
gazette/2000/05.04/radcliffe.html. See also Catalyst, *Two
Careers, One Marriage: Making It Work in the Workplace*
(New York: Catalyst, 1997).

8. Interview with Karol Rose by Meridith Levinson, "Flexible
Workplace: Lots of Talk, Little Action," CIO.com, June 5,
2008; retrieved February 22, 2010, from www.cio.com/

article/print/384064. See also Sally Thorton, "Five things I learned from the 'Flexibility: The Future of Work' Conference," Flexperience, n.d.; retrieved February 22, 2010, from www.flexperienceconsulting.com/index.php ?page=future-of-work-summary.

9. Women's Bureau, U.S. Department of Labor, *Flex-News*, no. 2, November 2009; retrieved March 17, 2010, from www.womenintech.com/flexnewsletternov.pdf.

10. Ellen Ernst Kossek and Brenda A. Lautsch, *CEO of Me: Creating a Life That Works in the Flexible Job Age* (Upper Saddle River, N.J.: Wharton School Publishing, 2008), p. 151.

11. Women's Bureau, U.S. Department of Labor, *Flex-News*, no. 2, November 2009.

12. Women's Bureau, U.S. Department of Labor, *Flex-News*, no. 2, November 2009.

13. Women's Bureau, U.S. Department of Labor, *Flex-News*, no. 2, November 2009.

14. Cali Yost, "Work+Life 'Fit' Tipping Point" (blog post) October 7, 2009; retrieved February 22, 2010, from http://worklifefit.com/blog/2009/10/worklife-fit-tipping -point/.

15. Ariane Hegewisch and Janet C. Gornick, "Statutory Routes to Workplace Flexibility in Cross-National Perspective," Washington, D.C.: Institute for Women's Policy Research, 2008; retrieved February 22, 2010, from www.lisproject.org/ publications/parentwork/FlexWorkReport.pdf.

16. "Leadership Through the Crisis and After: McKinsey Global Survey Results," *McKinsey Quarterly*, October 2009; retrieved March 15, 2010, from www.mckinseyquarterly .com/Leadership_through_the_crisis_and_after_McKinsey _Global_Survey_results_2457.

17. "Workplace Flexibility 2010, Public Policy Platform on Flexible Work Arrangements," Washington, D.C.: Georgetown University Law School, 2009; retrieved

February 22, 2010, from www.law.georgetown.edu/workplaceflexibility2010/definition/documents/PublicPolicyPlatformonFlexibleWorkArrangements.pdf.

18. Hegewisch and Gornick, "Statutory Routes to Workplace Flexibility in Cross-National Perspective."

19. The Working Families Flexibility Act (S.2419 and H.R. 4301), 110th Congress, introduced December 6, 2007; information retrieved February 22, 2010, from www.govtrack.us/congress/bill.xpd?bill=s110-2419.

20. Workplace Flexibility 2010, "A Comprehensive Public Policy Platform on Flexible Work Arrangements," n.d.; retrieved March 10, 2010, from www.law.georgetown.edu/workplaceflexibility2010/definition/FWAPublicPolicyPlatform.cfm.

Acknowledgments

The Custom-Fit Workplace was inspired by years of work and collaboration with a vibrant community of thinkers, organizers, workers, parents, and leaders. We count ourselves privileged to work with the MomsRising.org team and a host of policy partners, business leaders, scholars, and family members who have contributed to our ideas about the workplace and how to make it great.

We want to thank Leslie Miller, who helped us get the book researched and written, always with a special grace and unfailing sense of humor, even in the face of her own work-family challenges! Thanks also go to Jenna Free for helping us take the manuscript to the finish line. The editorial magic of these two experts from Girl Friday Productions (www.girlfridayproduction .com) was enormously helpful. We are deeply grateful to our editor at Jossey-Bass, Genoveva Llosa, for her unwavering commitment to the book's ideas and audience. Thanks also to the rest of the Jossey-Bass team and to Hilary Powers for her beautiful copyedits. Todd Shuster, our agent at Zachary Shuster Harmsworth, deserves special thanks for believing in the promise of a custom-fit workplace.

Thanks go to many people who answered our questions, shared their perspectives, read chapters, and cared for our children while we wrote the book: Richard Geruson, Wes Boyd, Matt Hendel, Brian Free, Kristin Rowe-Finkbeiner, Donna Norton, Mary Olivella, Joan Williams, Netsy Firestein, Maria Brandt, Sylvia Paul, Jane Grossman, Duncan Highsmith, Sue

Bingham, Joan Lester, Marc Fine, Robert Fuller, Carla Moquin, Ann Eastman, Rochelle Lefkowitz, Ann O'Leary, Vibhuti Mehra, Annie Snowbarger, Ellen Ernst Kossek, Marianne Betterly-Kohn, Gabriela Melano, Larry Boyd, Gail Boyd, Kate Munn, Juliana Barreto, and Kenia Vega.

We can't forget our families, who listened, advised, and tolerated the extra work part of our own work-life fit that created this book over the past year: Wes, Alec, and Robin; and Rich, Nathaniel, Luke, Joan, and Jake. Thanks for your insights, brainstorms, patience, and love.

Finally, we want to thank everyone we interviewed who shared their very personal and honest and sometimes painful stories with an eye toward making the workplace better for everyone.

About the Authors

Joan Blades is cofounder of two leading civic organizations: one-million-member MomsRising.org and five-million-member MoveOn.org—both virtual organizations that have no bricks-and-mortar headquarters. Also a business entrepreneur, Joan cofounded Berkeley Systems, a successful software company. Blades was nominated one of *Time* magazine's Most Influential People and has received numerous awards, including *Ms.* magazine's 2003 Woman of the Year Award and The Breast Cancer Fund's 2009 Hero Award. She is coauthor of *The Motherhood Manifesto* and author of *Mediate Your Divorce*.

Nanette Fondas, a Rhodes Scholar and doctor of business administration from Harvard Business School, has written extensively in the field of management, organizations, and work in both the popular press and scholarly journals. She is the winner of a best paper award from the Academy of Management, and her writing was recently featured in the "50 Visionaries" issue of *Utne Reader*. Formerly a professor at premier universities including Harvard's Radcliffe College, Duke's Fuqua School of Business, and the University of California, Nanette is currently executive editor at MomsRising and leads the workplace flexibility initiative. She also writes frequently in national newspapers, magazines, and blogs about innovative ideas to make U.S. policies and business practices more employee- and family-friendly. She lives in Silicon Valley, California, with her husband and four children.

Index